SOMERSET CANALS

HENRY BUCKTON

AMBERLEY

First published 2026

Amberley Publishing
The Hill, Stroud,
Gloucestershire, GL5 4EP

www.amberley-books.com

ISBN: 978 1 3981 3118 7 (print)
ISBN: 978 1 3981 3119 4 (ebook)

British Library Cataloguing in Publication Data.
A catalogue record for this book is available from the British Library.

Typeset in 10pt on 13pt Celeste.
Typesetting by Hurix Digital, India.
Printed in the UK.

Appointed GPSR EU Representative: Easy Access System Europe Oü, 16879218
Address: Mustamäe tee 50, 10621, Tallinn, Estonia
Contact Details: gpsr.requests@easproject.com, +358 40 500 3575

Contents

Introduction

At the start of the eighteenth century Somerset remained almost entirely rural, and the towns and villages within its borders were linked by a network of very rudimentary roads that were little more than dirt tracks. As these towns began to grow and new industries

Plan from 1811 showing the present and projected navigable communications in the county of Somerset including, the Kennet and Avon Canal, the Grand Western Canal, the Bristol and Taunton Canal and the Somersetshire Coal Canal. (Photo © bathintime.co.uk/Bath and North East Somerset Council)

emerged within them, a better system of transport was required to both bring to the factories the raw materials they needed for their individual purposes, such as coal and metal ores, but also to ferry the goods they manufactured to the wider world. It was from this situation that the golden age of canals in Great Britain was born. Canals were of huge significance to the growth of the country's economy and status, and their ability to facilitate the bulk movement of these raw materials was one of the key factors in the success of the Industrial Revolution.

Somerset, similar to many other English counties, would benefit from several schemes. Goods from places as varied as Bath, Taunton, Chard and Glastonbury could be moved to coastal ports like Bridgwater, Highbridge and Bristol by a series of artificial waterways. Although these canals proved to be hugely successful, their importance was short-lived, as by the end of the nineteenth century they had been almost entirely superseded by the railways.

Although Somerset's canals would be largely abandoned and forgotten, and in some cases reclaimed by nature, many would be rediscovered in the twentieth century and renovated. Because of this we are now able to walk or cycle along the routes of their towpaths and in some cases even operate barges on them again for recreational purposes.

In this book I will relate short histories of all the county's examples, including the Bridgwater and Taunton Canal, the Kennet and Avon Canal and the Grand Western Canal. These and other examples are still evident in the landscape and provide us with a fascinating glimpse into Somerset's industrial heritage.

1

Kennet and Avon Canal

We begin in the very north of the county with the Kennet and Avon Canal, which, at the time it opened in 1811, was the culmination of several schemes aimed at linking Bristol in the west to London in the east – in other words, a navigable waterway that cut straight through southern England. Before this there were two options available for moving goods from coast to coast. The first was over land using pack mules, or horses, and carts. This option was very slow, negotiated along uneven roads that often involved paying expensive turnpike tolls, with the amounts that could be carried relatively small. The second option was a lengthy sea journey down the Bristol Channel, around Cornwall and through the English Channel to the mouth of the River Thames. More cargo could be transported this way, but the passage was fraught with danger. It was a wild and often stormy coast, with many of the fragile wooden ships being smashed against rocks, shipwrecked and plundered by gangs of wreckers. It was also a time when Great Britain was at war with France, which meant that ships passing through the English Channel ran the risk of being attacked by French warships, privateers or even pirates.

In the early eighteenth century, work had been carried out that would unknowingly have a direct impact on the later creation of the Kennet and Avon Canal. The River Kennet had been made navigable between Newbury and Reading, from where it linked into the River Thames. This navigation was opened for business in 1723. Meanwhile, in the west the River Avon had also been made navigable between Bristol and Bath, with that navigation opening in 1727.

With these two river navigations in place, it was soon realised that if a canal was dug between them, it would provide that much longed for link between Bristol and London. When finished, the Kennet and Avon Canal would be 87 miles long. The name refers to the entire watercourse, comprising both the two sections of navigable rivers and the central man-made section. The central section between Bath and Newbury was dug between 1794 and 1810 and was 57 miles in length. The entire watercourse would incorporate 105 locks, most spectacularly the Caen Hill flight near Devizes.

Plans for the canal began to formalise in 1788 when politicians and business leaders sought to improve trade and communication links between towns like Marlborough and Chippenham. At that time the proposal was given the name of the Western Canal, although

Bath Bottom Lock on the Kennet and Avon Canal, pictured in April 1969. (Photo courtesy of Railway and Canal Historical Society: Dennis Hadley Collection)

Moorings close to Keynsham Lock, near the Lock Keeper pub. The lock opened on the Bristol Avon Navigation in 1727. (Photo © Hugh Llewelyn)

it was later changed to the Kennet and Avon Canal in order to avoid confusion with the Grand Western Canal, which was also being proposed around the same time between Taunton and Tiverton. The Kennet and Avon Canal Company was subsequently created to deal with the canal's business under the chairmanship of Charles Dundas, who was the Member of Parliament for Berkshire.

In 1789, engineers Barnes, Simcock and Weston carried out a favourable feasibility study of taking the canal along this slightly northern route. Later, however, there were concerns that this particular course would suffer from a lack of a suitable water supply. So, in 1793, a new study was made by John Rennie, a Scottish civil engineer who already had a great deal of experience in designing and building canals, having previously worked on projects including the Lancaster Canal and the Chelmer and Blackwater Navigation.

Rennie examined a more southerly route going from Bath to Newbury through Devizes, which was considered more achievable. This was the route that was eventually adopted by the company, who thereafter set about raising the necessary funds by taking subscriptions from prospective shareholders.

On 17 April 1794, the Kennet and Avon Canal Act was passed through Parliament, receiving what was termed 'royal assent', and John Rennie was appointed consulting engineer. This meant that work was now able to start. By which time a group of

Dundas Aqueduct, named after Charles Dundas, the first chairman of the Kennet and Avon Canal Company. (Illustration by Jean Claude Nattes, from *Bath Illustrated by a Series of Views* published in 1805; photo © bathintime.co.uk/Bath Record Office: Archives and Local Studies)

businessmen from Bristol who had taken over the management of the canal project had raised £264,000 in share subscriptions.

The 57-mile-long central section of the canal was finished in 1810 and the whole system was opened for barge traffic in early 1811. It was a revolutionary project which allowed for the safe movement of varied cargos between the River Severn at Bristol and the River Thames through London. It was also without doubt one of the most aesthetically impressive canal systems to be built anywhere in Britain, with a series of classical bridges and aqueducts. The final cost of this ambitious undertaking was estimated at around £1,072,000. This was a huge amount of money in the early nineteenth century, but the wealth it helped to generate to its customers at the height of the Industrial Revolution is incalculable.

Although the canal didn't completely open for traffic until 1811, certain sections were being used as early as 1801 while the system was still under construction. A perfect example of this on the Somerset section was at the Dundas Aqueduct to the south-east of Bath, near Monkton Combe, which opened in 1805, carrying the canal across the River Avon and into the neighbouring county of Wiltshire. It was here, at the same time, that a link was made to the Somerset Coal Canal. Although the Kennet and Avon Canal itself was

The Kennet and Avon was one of the most aesthetically pleasing canals in Britain, having a series of classical aqueducts and bridges such as these in Bath's Sydney Gardens. (Illustration by Jean Claude Nattes, from *Bath Illustrated by a Series of Views* published in 1805; photo: © bathintime.co.uk/Bath and North East Somerset Council)

still not completed along its entire length by this time, it meant that large shipments of coal from the Somerset Coalfield could now be transported on the waterway to Bath and Bristol. At Dundas Wharf you can still see the tollhouse, a warehouse and a crane used by the company as lasting reminders of the canal's past.

When the canal was finally finished, the cost of using it for the barge owners was extremely favourable in comparison with carriage by road. In order to navigate the entire watercourse from Bath to London, it would cost around £3 per ton, compared with anywhere between £6 and £7 per ton using the roads. Because of this factor alone, the canal proved very successful from the outset.

By 1812 it was clear to the Kennet and Avon Canal Company that it would be better for all concerned if they owned the entire system, not merely the central section between Bath and Newbury that they had built themselves. With this in mind, the Kennet and Avon Canal Company and River Kennet Navigation Act 1813 was passed through Parliament. This Act authorised them to purchase the Kennet Navigation, which stretched from Newbury to the junction with the Thames near Reading for a cost of £100,000. The money for this was raised through the sale of 5,500 shares at £24 each. In 1816, the company was also able to purchase a major shareholding in the Avon Navigation, which ultimately gave them almost total control over the entire length of the watercourse.

A significant location in the Somerset stretch of the canal was at Claverton, where it cut into the side of the Avon Valley, 48 feet above the River Avon. Here, in order to overcome water supply issues, John Rennie built a pumping station between 1809 and 1813. Water was diverted from the river at Warleigh Weir to the pumping station along a 30-foot-wide leat. At the station, an enormous waterwheel, 24 feet in diameter, powered a large beam engine that would pump 50 gallons of water every two seconds from the river up to the canal.

This photograph from *c.* 1910 shows an event of some sort taking place at Dundas Wharf. (Photo © bathintime.co.uk/Bath Record Office: Archives and Local Studies)

The pumping station remained working right up until 1952 and was largely unaltered throughout its working life. For some time it lay derelict, until between 1969 and 1976 volunteers restored it. Today it is maintained and run by the Claverton Pumping Station Trust and is open for public visits on specified days.

At Bathwick, two important structures are the Sydney Gardens tunnels, both of which were designed by John Rennie and constructed between 1800 and 1810. The gardens were laid out in the early 1790s as a commercial pleasure garden with a variety of attractions, just before the arrival of the canal. The canal company and the proprietors of the gardens came to an arrangement that allowed the watercourse to go through the gardens as long as the canal company provided tunnels and ornamental bridges at their expense. Consequently, No. 1 Tunnel, which was also known as the Cleveland Tunnel, carried the canal into Sydney Gardens from the south. It was approximately 177 feet long. No. 2 Tunnel, known as the Sydney Gardens Tunnel, took the canal out of the gardens to the north and was around 167 feet in length. Standing over the No. 1 Tunnel is Cleveland House, built in the late 1810s. It would be used by the Kennet and Avon Canal Company as their headquarters between 1825 and 1864.

The canal's course through the city of Bath required the building of several locks, which now number six, although there were originally seven. Bath Bottom Lock, also known as Widcombe Lock, was seventh on the whole system, the first being Hanham Lock, which was actually on the Avon Navigation to the east of Bristol's floating harbour. Bath Bottom Lock can be found at the point where the canal joins the River Avon, just to the south of Pulteney Bridge. Near the lock is a side pond and pumping station which pumps water through the locks to replace that which is used every time the lock is opened.

Next is Bath Deep Lock, which comprises what had been two locks, Nos 8 and 9. These were combined during restoration work in 1976. Its chamber is 19 feet and 5 inches deep,

Archive image of Claverton Pumping Station, which was built between 1809 and 1813. (Photo © Claverton Pumping Station)

Some of the working machinery inside Claverton Pumping Station, where water was pumped from the River Avon up to the canal, some 48 feet above. (Photo © Claverton Pumping Station)

Cleveland House stands over No. 1 Tunnel as it passes through Sydney Gardens in Bath. It was used by the Kennet and Avon Canal Company as their headquarters between 1825 and 1864. This photograph dates from around 1950. (Photo © bathintime.co.uk/Bath and North East Somerset Council)

making it the second-deepest canal lock in Great Britain. The other locks in succession are Wash House Lock (No. 10), Abbey View Lock (No. 11), Pulteney Lock (No. 12) and Bath Top Lock (No. 13).

As the years passed, barges became more and more efficient, and by 1818 there are said to have been at least seventy vessels working daily on the canal, each with the ability to carry 60 tons of cargo. An average journey between Bath and Newbury would take around three-and-a-half days to complete. At this time coal and quarried stone made up the bulk of tonnage being ferried, which by 1832 amounted to around 300,000 tons of freight a year. As for its worth, between 1825 and 1834 the company had an annual revenue of around £45,000.

Unfortunately, the boom days for the canal didn't last long, as the opening of the Great Western Railway in 1841 offered a cheaper and faster alternative for the carriage of goods. In response, the company lowered its tariffs, but it was all in vain and in 1852 the railway company bought the canal and took over its running. It spent very little on maintenance and restricted the canal's operation. For instance, from 1861 traffic was prohibited on the canal at night, while from 1865 boats had to use the locks in pairs to reduce water loss. Annual tonnage fell from 360,610 tons in 1848 to 210,567 tons in 1868. In 1877, the canal recorded a deficit of £1,920.

This photograph from 2006 shows barges in Bath Deep Lock, which is the second-deepest canal lock in Great Britain. It was originally two locks. (Photo © Don Cload)

Things worsened in 1904 and 1906 with the closures of the Somerset Coal Canal and the Wilts and Berks Canal, respectively, both of which had been major suppliers through the system. Then, after suffering further losses, in 1925 the Great Western Railway decided that enough was enough and sought to completely close the canal by obtaining a Ministry of Transport Order. This was refused, however, and the company was told to improve its maintenance of the canal. Although freight through the system continued to decline, pleasure boats began to appear on the water, which in a sense offered a tantalising glimpse of the future.

It would prove wise to keep the canal open at this time as it would find itself featuring as a component of national security during the Second World War. Rivers and canals became crucial to defence plans in the event that the Germans invaded the country along the south coast and marched north from there. Rivers and canals would all have to be crossed by the enemy troops as they advanced, so they became important to a series of 'stop lines' put in place to halt the invaders. The Kennet and Avon Canal was part of what was known as the GHQ Line – Blue. In 1940, a series of heavily armed concrete pillboxes was built at regular intervals along its northern bank.

Happily, the invasion never transpired and after the war the Transport Act 1947 transferred control of the canal to the British Transport Commission. Nevertheless, the decline continued and in the 1950s, mainly due to poor maintenance of the locks, large sections of the system had to be closed, even to pleasure craft. The last through passage was made in 1951.

The Kennet and Avon Canal from Abbey View Lock, Bath, reproduced from a postcard published in the Pelham Series by Boots, probably early twentieth century. (Author's collection)

Postcard showing Pulteney Lock on the Kennet and Avon Canal, *c.* 1900. (Author's collection)

In March 1956, the British Transport Commission attempted to pass an Act through Parliament that would remove the right of navigation between Bath and Reading. This was vigorously opposed by interested parties all along the length of the canal, and a petition with 22,000 signatures was brought from Bristol to London in a canoe via navigable waterways, including sections of the canal, where it was presented to the queen.

This campaign led to an inquiry by a Parliamentary Select Committee, which ultimately agreed with suspending the right of navigation and the Act was subsequently passed through the House of Commons. However, this was amended by the House of Lords to include a clause that would prevent any further deterioration of the canal, thus keeping everyone's hopes of preserving it alive. Subsequently, the Bowes Committee was tasked with looking into the situation further, not just on the Kennet and Avon Canal but on all navigable waterways.

In July 1958, the committee published the results of their inquiry into Inland Waterways, which in the case of the Kennet and Avon Canal concluded that there was no justification for restoring the section between Bath and Reading. However, a year later in 1959, a government white paper turned things around again and recommended the establishment of an Inland Waterways Redevelopment Advisory Committee. Their brief was to assist schemes designed at regenerating canals that were no longer able to finance their own maintenance. The Kennet and Avon Canal was a beneficiary of this scheme and in 1962 the Advisory Committee agreed it should be redeveloped, allocating £20,000 for its maintenance with a further £20,000 to fund the start of the restoration work.

Two narrowboats moored outside the George Inn at Bathampton on the Kennet and Avon Canal in 2011. (Photo © Stephen McKay)

The group that had been largely responsible for promoting the restoration of the canal was called the Kennet and Avon Canal Association. In 1962, they became the Kennet and Avon Canal Trust and were given the responsibility of restoring the system between Bristol and Reading, both as a through navigation and as a public amenity. In April of that year, they gained charitable status and in June 1962, they were incorporated under the Companies Act. In 1963, the Transport Act replaced the British Transport Commission with the newly formed British Waterways as the statutory body for inland waterways. In partnership with the Kennet and Avon Canal Trust and local authorities along the watercourse, British Waterways took responsibility for the canal's affairs and restoration work began in earnest all along the course of the canal in the early 1970s, with the lower Widcombe locks in Bath reopened in 1973.

The overall restoration would take around twenty years to complete and the canal was reopened by Queen Elizabeth II on 8 August 1990, allowing pleasure craft to once again operate along its entire route. It had been a huge effort between British Waterways and the Kennet and Avon Canal Trust, with gangs of volunteers working largely at weekends. As skilled as the volunteers proved to be, the work often required the expertise of professional contractors, leaving the volunteers to fundraise for the vast amounts of money required. In 1996, the National Lottery awarded its biggest ever single grant from the Heritage Lottery Fund – £25,000,000 – to help with ongoing work and make the canal sustainable and accessible for the enjoyment of future generations.

The reopening of the Kennet and Avon Canal's lower Widcombe locks in Bath, 1973. (Photo © bathintime.co.uk/Bath and North East Somerset Council)

Volunteers of the Claverton Pumping Station Trust working hard maintaining machinery at the historic site. (Photo © Claverton Pumping Station)

2

Somerset Coal Canal

During the Industrial Revolution coal became increasingly in demand at mills and factories all around the country for running some of the new steam-powered machinery. North Somerset had coal in abundance, with it dug out of a huge coalfield that covered an area of around 240 square miles. However, getting it to the end users was not an easy task as North Somerset had very few roads at that time. Instead, it was crossed by little more than a network of narrow lanes and droves, which had historically been used by farmers to move their herds to pasture and market.

Initially the coal was carried in panniers by horses, though this proved to be very slow and the quantities that could be transported were only small. By the middle of the eighteenth century, turnpike roads made things a little easier as wagons pulled by horses or mules could now be used on much-improved highways, but they were expensive for the mining companies to use. So, dissatisfied with this situation, as well as the costs involved, the owners of several coal mines decided to form a committee to look into the possibility of building a canal to carry the coal away from the coalfield to Bath, Bristol and Wiltshire.

Initial surveys of a possible route were made in 1793 under the direction of John Rennie, who, of course, was also involved with the Kennet and Avon Canal at that time. He appointed William Jessop, another engineer with significant experience in canal building, and William Smith to carry out the survey.

William Smith, who would later become the official surveyor to the Somerset Coal Canal, had been employed at Mearns Pit at High Littleton when he first observed and recorded the various layers of rock and coal exposed by mining. This subsequently led to the formation of his theories of stratigraphy and earned him the nickname William 'Strata' Smith. In fact, Smith was credited with creating the very first detailed, nationwide geological map of Great Britain and is today regarded as the father of English geology.

Smith and Jessop presented their report to the committee on 14 October 1793, estimating the cost of the canal's construction at around £80,000. In 1794, the Somersetshire Coal Canal Act was passed through Parliament, after which further detailed surveys were carried out by Robert Whitworth and John Sutcliffe, the latter then being appointed as chief engineer.

The Somerset Coal Canal, which was originally known as the Somersetshire Coal Canal, was planned to have two branches. The first, in the north, would begin in basins at Paulton

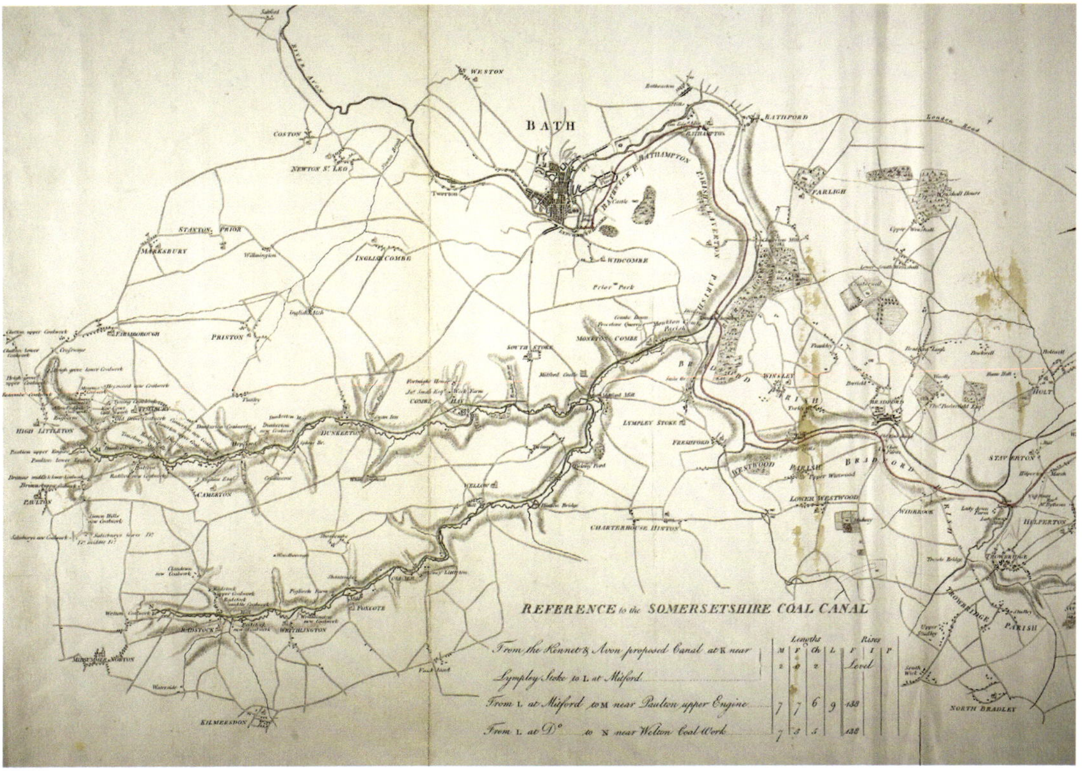

Plan from 1793 of the proposed navigable canal between the River Kennet at Newbury and the River Avon at Bath, to which is added a plan of the proposed Somersetshire Coal Canal. Surveyed by John Rennie and engraved by W. Faden, Geographer to King George III. (Photo © bathintime.co.uk/Bath Record Office: Archives and Local Studies)

View of Camerton New Pit which was operational on the Somerset coalfield and closed in 1950. The line of the Somerset Coal Canal can be clearly seen on the left of the picture. (Photo courtesy of Radstock Museum)

and Timsbury and then run to nearby Camerton. From there it would pass over two aqueducts at Dunkerton, through a tunnel at Combe Hay and then join up to the second branch at Midford. It would roughly follow the course of a river called the Cam Brook, from which it originally took its water through a pumping station at Dunkerton.

The second branch, in the south, would start at Radstock and run through a tunnel at Wellow before converging with the first branch at Midford. This arm would loosely follow a local watercourse known as the Wellow Brook. From Midford, the combined canal would finally connect to the Kennet and Avon Canal at Brassknocker Basin on the Dundas Aqueduct, near Monkton Combe. This link would not only give the coalfield access to Bath, Bristol and the waterways of Wiltshire, as initially intended, but an eastwards link to the London markets as well.

Work began on the northern branch of the canal in June 1795 after a review was made of various tenders that had been submitted to the committee. They eventually chose a firm called Houghton & Son to complete the project, who, despite being based in Shropshire, would use local labour to carry out the work. Their first task was to construct the terminus at Timsbury Basin, from where the whole operation would commence. This was located in some meadows downstream of Gooseyard Bridge, opposite the Paulton Engine Iron Foundry, which is now a private residence but at the time provided much of the metal infrastructure for the coalfield in general. The route would proceed from there to a place called Hopyard, in the parish of Camerton, a distance of around 2 miles.

The Somerset Coal Canal at Brassknocker Basin, *c.* 1904. The Viaduct Inn is seen in the background. The inn closed in 2005 and is now in residential use. (Photo © bathintime.co.uk/ Peter Dafnis)

In time, the wharf at Timsbury Basin would include various storage sheds, stables and a wharfinger's cottage. The wharfinger was an official who would take custody of and be responsible for goods delivered to the wharf and have responsibility for its day-to-day running.

Aound 100 yards downstream of Timsbury Basin was another wharf, which served traffic arriving from the various coal mines around Paulton. This site was known as Paulton Basin. Before long some fifteen separate collieries around Timsbury and Paulton were connected to these two basins alone, each having access to their own, or a shared, tramway.

Once the terminus and link to Camerton were completed, the section between Camerton and Dunkerton was excavated. In fact, this was the first stretch of the canal to be filled with water. Keen to get things rolling, the company tested five coal boats here on 1 October 1798. At Dunkerton, the loads were removed from the water and loaded onto carts to be taken along the turnpike road to Bath pulled by horses. A wharf was hurriedly completed at Dunkerton in November of that same year, and from that time forth was used by at least two carts a day to take coal loads to Bath, while the rest of the canal was still under construction.

All of this also required the building of three bridges to carry the trams from the collieries across the Cam Brook. Further along the canal, beyond the basins, more tramways were connected to it, leading from Withy Mills and the Radford workings. This also required the building of another bridge at Upper Radford. In some places, in order to protect the

Repaired bridge at Paulton Basin over a dry dock on the Somerset Coal Canal, which allowed towpath access onto the wharf. (Photo © Rick Crowley)

integrity of the canal, the actual course of the Cam Brook had to be slightly modified. Also, a few of these tramway connections, including the one from Withy Mills, required the building of inclines to carry the coal down steep slopes to the canal below.

With coal already being ferried to Dunkerton and delivered to Bath, it was now time to concentrate on the next section of the canal, between Dunkerton and Midford. However, here there was a serious logistical problem: because of the hilly terrain, there was a drop of 135 feet between the two. In order to proceed, this would require the building of a number of locks, the main concentration of which would be around Combe Hay.

It was initially decided to use what were known as caisson locks, as opposed to standard conventional locks. In the operation of a caisson lock, a narrowboat would be floated into a sealed watertight box and raised or lowered between the water levels of the canal. This was intended to solve the problem of requiring excessive amounts of water when conventional locks were used to raise and lower boats between large water height differences.

The inventor of the caisson lock at Combe Hay was Robert Weldon at the time his design was already undergoing trials on the Shropshire Canal. Construction of the first of these locks began in 1796 and was complete and ready for testing between November 1797 and June 1798. The masonry chamber, known as the cistern, was 81 feet long and 20 feet wide, and had a depth of 61 feet and 6 inches. The wooden caisson, or moving box within the cistern, was 80 feet long, 10 feet and 6 inches wide and 11 feet and 6 inches tall.

Humpbacked bridge over the canal bed at Midford. (Photo © Guy Wareham)

The entrance to one of the derelict locks on the Somerset Coal Canal at Combe Hay. (Photo © Guy Wareham)

It was designed to provide a lift of 46 feet. If it was successful, only three of these locks would be needed instead of the estimated twenty-two conventional locks that were initially perceived for the project.

Unfortunately, the first attempted descent failed and was subsequently followed by several other attempts with mixed results. Some did seem to work, with others floundering. In the end, frustrated with the whole process, not to mention the costly lack of progress, on 22 August 1799 the caisson locks were finally abandoned.

Weldon's design was eventually replaced by a planned system of three locks and a section of tramway along an inclined plane. An inclined plane was essentially a section of the canal that is out of water; the barges would be placed in caissons and pulled along a stretch of rails before being put back into the water again at the other end. However, this didn't appear to work either, so a flight of nineteen locks was suggested instead. Unfortunately, by now the finances of the canal company were under pressure and in order to pay for this they had to raise more money. In doing so it would mean that an additional toll of 1*s* per ton would have to be levied on all canal traffic. This was vigorously opposed by the people who would be using the canal, most notably the owners of the Kennet and Avon Canal and the Wilts and Berks Canal on the grounds that the price of the coal to their customers would be far too high.

Following lengthy negotiations, the company eventually obtained a new Act of Parliament on 30 April 1802 that authorised the formation of a separate body called the Lock Fund of the Somerset Coal Canal Company. This Act gave the company licence to raise the sum of £45,000, which would be provided by the Kennet and Avon Canal, the Wilts and Berks

The dry chambers of locks 14, 13 and 12 on the Somerset Coal Canal at Combe Hay. (Photo © Guy Wareham)

Photograph of the Somerset Coal Canal at Tucking Mill in the 1890s, with a team of four horses pulling a cart loaded with stone or wood. The canal and towpath are clearly visible on the left-hand side. (Photo courtesy of Radstock Museum)

Canal and the Somerset Coal Canal, each contributing £15,000. The 1*s* surcharge would then be levied until the capital had been repaid, after which it would cease.

In the end, the original plan – for twenty-two conventional locks – was seen through to completion, as everything else seemed to be either unsuitable or unworkable. These successfully raised the canal the required 135 feet over approximately 1½ miles. The finished lock flight opened in 1805, allowing the Somerset Coal Canal to finally link into the Kennet and Avon Canal at Brassknocker Basin on the Dundas Aqueduct. The locks would remain in operation until 1899. Interestingly, if you visit Brassknocker Basin today, this short stretch of the canal is still in water and features boat moorings, cycle hire and a café.

Before entering the Kennet and Avon Canal, every barge had to be weighed. This was done at Midford where a weigh house was specially built for the purpose in 1831. The barges would be floated into a one-ended lock, the gate closed and the water drained. This left the boat resting on a cradle suspended by angled rods attached to a beam, which took the weight of the boat and recorded it. This weigh house was apparently one of just four known to have been built in England and Wales.

Before long the northern branch of the Somerset Coal Canal was proving to be a great success. The best year it recorded was in 1838 when 138,403 tons of coal was transported along it, resulting in over £17,000 of tolls being paid. Annual cargos of over 100,000 tons were not uncommon right up until the 1870s, when the decline in output of coal from the various Somerset coal mines, along with competition from the railways, dramatically reduced the canal's profitability.

Barges moored at Brassknocker Basin at the end of the Somerset Coal Canal. (Photo © Eirian Evans)

Although the northern branch of the canal was proving profitable, the southern branch from Radstock, linking the collieries in that area to the canal basin at Midford some 7¼ miles away, was never actually completed. Although one lock was built, as well as the tunnel at Wellow and an aqueduct over the brook, the company decided to stop construction in order to avoid the expense of building any further locks. Before the work was stopped the canal had been dug as far as Twinhoe, from where a tramway was then laid to take the coal the rest of the way to Midford.

In 1815, it was deemed more profitable to abandon the canal idea totally and continue the horse-drawn tramway all along the towpath instead. This was a single-line tramway with passing places every 600 yards and was originally laid using cast-iron plates on stone block sleepers and later re-laid using wrought-iron plates. Apparently, teams of three horses would haul eight or nine wagons along the towpath, each weighing around 11 hundredweights. The Radstock tramway and the northern branch of the canal would converge over an aqueduct at Midford, where all the coal would be loaded onto barges for onward transportation.

By the 1880s, coal production had declined right across the Somerset Coalfield, as several mines either ran out of workable coal or were flooded. In 1896, the main pump at Dunkerton, which maintained the water level in the canal, failed and the company could not afford to replace it. The resultant lowering in water level meant that only small loads could now be transported, which greatly reduced the company's revenue.

However, this was all to be academic anyway, as before long the process of moving coal would be taken over by the railways, at first the Bristol & North Somerset Railway and later

The weigh house at Midford, *c.* 1890. (Photo courtesy of Radstock Museum)

the Somerset & Dorset Joint Railway. The canal became disused around 1898 and officially closed in 1902. After that most of it was drained for reasons of safety. The locks, aqueducts and other structures slowly fell into disrepair and some disappeared altogether beneath dense vegetation, lost and forgotten.

In 1991, the Somersetshire Coal Canal Society was formed with the aim of preserving and conserving the canal. In 2000, volunteers from the society began to uncover and restore some of the lock flight around Combe Hay. In 2002, a £700,000 Heritage Lottery Fund grant enabled the restoration of the Grade II-listed Midford Aqueduct, which was an important link between the two branches of the canal. The work at Combe Hay was expanded to the remaining lock flight in 2011, as landowner permission needed to be sought before this could commence. All the work has been undertaken alongside the Inland Waterways Association's Waterway Recovery Group and is ongoing.

Midford Aqueduct where the Radstock branch of the Somerset Coal Canal crossed the Cam Brook before meeting up with the Paulton branch. (Photo © Guy Wareham)

The pumping station at Dunkerton which pumped water from Cam Brook into the Somerset Coal Canal. (Photo courtesy of Radstock Museum)

3

Dorset and Somerset Canal

The Dorset and Somerset Canal was a proposed waterway that would cut through south-west England and have an important branch in North Somerset. However, for various reasons it was never actually completed, although scant reminders of the section that was built can still be found in the countryside between Frome and the Nettlebridge Valley. It was one of several schemes discussed during the eighteenth and nineteenth centuries that aimed to link the Bristol Channel and the English Channel without having to sail around Cornwall. This was for the same reasons we noted when discussing the Kennet and Avon Canal Company's plan to link the Bristol Channel with the Thames Estuary via an overland route, thus avoiding the many dangers posed by the alternative seaward passage.

Original plans for the scheme began to emerge around 1792 when local captains of industry and politicians began to give the idea serious consideration. One of the most influential of these was James Fussell IV, whose family ran a series of iron mills on the banks of the Mells River in the Wadbury Valley, between the villages of Mells and Great Elm. Here, during the Industrial Revolution, the Fussell family ran a highly successful business producing edge tools such as scythes, sickles, spades, shovels, billhooks and other agricultural implements. The business was first established in 1744 by James Fussell III, on the site of an earlier works that had been run by a certain James Naylor.

Iron ore was not actually smelted at these sites but brought in as scrap or pig iron, although there is some evidence to suggest that steel was made here. The iron brought into the valley was used to produce a range of tools that were being exported throughout Europe and North America. The business was further developed by Fussell's son, James Fussell IV, who became an avid promoter of the Dorset and Somerset Canal. We can clearly see how access to a nearby canal would have been hugely beneficial to the iron industry here, especially as roads suitable for carrying large cargos of metal and coal were practically non-existent.

A public meeting was held in Wincanton in January 1793 when the committee, who were promoting the idea, gave an outline of the plan and sought financial backing from would-be subscribers. The original route that was suggested would run between Poole on the Dorset coast and a spot on the River Avon, near Bath. On the way it would pass through or close to Wareham, Sturminster Newton, Wincanton and Frome. There would also be a

Whatcombe Wall, an increasingly tall stone wall which faced a section of the Dorset and Somerset Canal embankment. It can still be seen today and is often referred to as the 'Roman Wall'. (Photo courtesy of Derrick Hunt)

branch of the canal going through the Nettlebridge Valley to serve the many coal mines in that area.

The majority of the pits on the Somerset Coalfield could be found around the town of Radstock, the village of Farrington Gurney and the Cam Brook, Wellow Brook and Nettlebridge valleys. As we have already seen, the Somerset Coal Canal, which was being planned around the same time, served collieries near the courses of the Cam Brook and Wellow Brook, which left those in the Nettlebridge Valley somewhat isolated and forgotten. So, this scheme, if it went ahead, would have been a massive boost to their productivity.

In the first instance the canal engineer Robert Whitworth was asked to survey a possible route. He reported back to the committee in September 1793, suggesting that the route of the main line of the canal should now begin with a link to the Kennet and Avon Canal at Freshford, rather than as initially planned by joining the River Avon near Bath. From Freshford it would now head towards Blandford, instead of Wareham. These changes in the route were necessitated because of the principal requirement of any canal system, which was the availability of a nearby adequate water supply.

Robert Whitworth was in great demand at the time, having worked on many canal projects in England previously. In 1794, he was involved with surveying a route for the Somerset Coal Canal among other things. So, finding himself too busy to provide his services to the Dorset and Somerset project, he recommended that the promoters of the scheme should employ Frome-based engineer William Bennet as a suitable replacement to take things further.

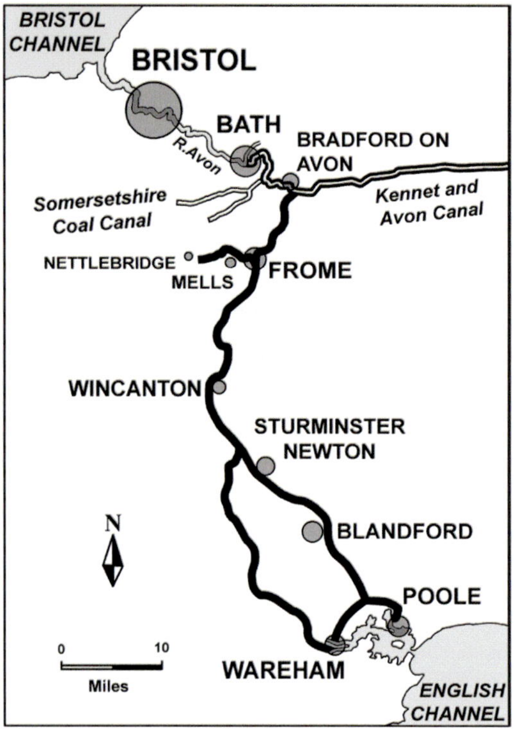

Map showing the intended route of the Dorset and Somerset Canal from the Bristol Channel to the English Channel, including the branch from Frome to Nettlebridge. (Photo courtesy of Derrick Hunt)

Near the Duke of Cumberland pub in the hamlet of Edford is Edford Bridge, a packhorse bridge built over the canal. The underside of the arch has been infilled to prevent its collapse. (Photo courtesy of Derrick Hunt)

At the time Bennet was also busy working on plans for the Ivelchester and Langport Navigation, another canal project taking place in the county concurrently, so he was unable to complete a detailed survey for the Dorset and Somerset Canal route until the middle of 1795. His plan was largely agreed by the committee, except for the point at which the system would join the Kennet and Avon Canal. He suggested they should meet at the Dundas Aqueduct, but the committee asked him to relook at this and in his final survey, which was submitted on 13 August 1795, the joining point was moved to Widbrook, near Bradford-on-Avon.

Bennet estimated the cost of building the canal to be around £200,000, which would also include short branches to Hamworthy and Wareham. In a bid to reduce the cost, the southern end, which had been intended to go all the way to Poole, was cut back to Shillingstone, where it could link into the River Stour for onward movement to the English Channel. He presented detailed evidence illustrating the engineering aspects of the entire project, which enabled the committee to obtain the necessary Act of Parliament on 24 March 1796. The Act gave what had now become the Dorset and Somerset Canal Company the power to raise £150,000, with an additional £75,000 if they required it. However, for various reasons, less than £80,000 was actually raised. Undeterred and in order to capitalise on the lucrative markets in the coal fields and the cloth mills of Frome, the company decided to plough ahead and work began on the Somerset branch in September 1796.

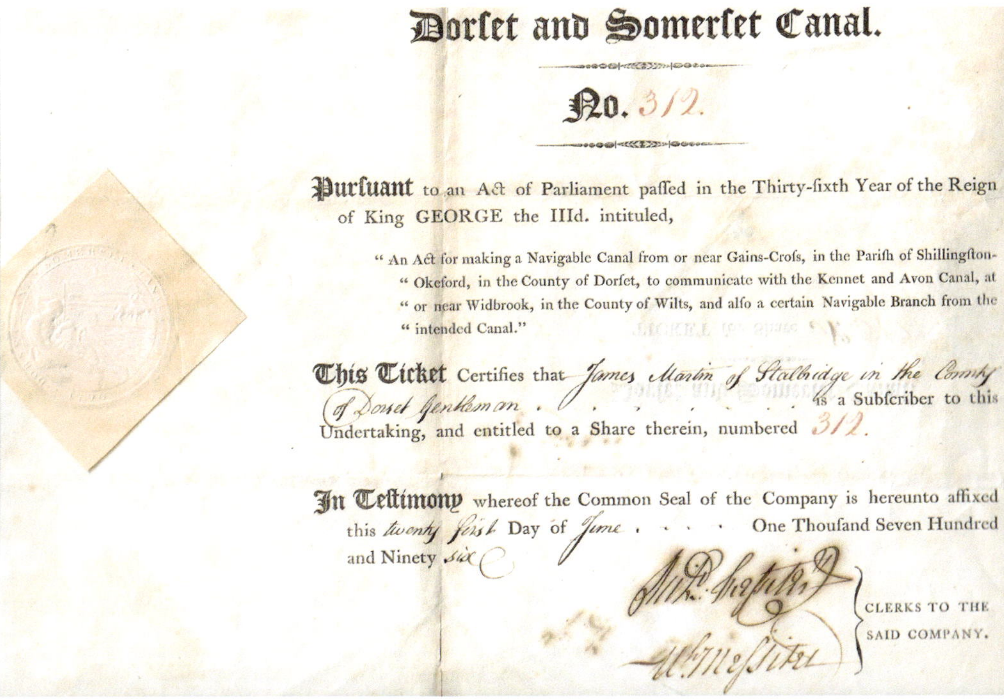

Dorfet and Somerfet Canal.

No. 312.

Purfuant to an Act of Parliament paffed in the Thirty-fixth Year of the Reign of King GEORGE the IIId. intituled,

"An Act for making a Navigable Canal from or near Gains-Crofs, in the Parifh of Shillingfton-"Okeford, in the County of Dorfet, to communicate with the Kennet and Avon Canal, at "or near Widbrook, in the County of Wilts, and alfo a certain Navigable Branch from the "intended Canal."

This Ticket Certifies that James Martin of Stalbridge in the County of Dorset Gentleman . . . . is a Subfcriber to this Undertaking, and entitled to a Share therein, numbered 312.

In Teftimony whereof the Common Seal of the Company is hereunto affixed this twenty first Day of June . . . . One Thoufand Seven Hundred and Ninety six

CLERKS TO THE SAID COMPANY.

Share certificate issued to subscribers to the Dorset and Somerset Canal undertaking dated 21 June 1796. This example is ticket No. 312, issued to James Martin of Stalbridge. (Photo courtesy of Derrick Hunt)

Since November 1795, Bennet had also been working as an engineer for the Somerset Coal Canal, so he was well aware of the system of caisson locks being built by Robert Weldon around Combe Hay. His scheme for the Frome branch of the Dorset and Somerset Canal would include a similar system and although construction had begun, he deferred any work on the locks until the results were known regarding the trials on the neighbouring project. As we know, that didn't end well and Weldon's design was scrapped and ultimately replaced by conventional locks.

There were 8 miles of the new canal duly built from Stratton Common towards Frome, passing through Coleford and Vobster. This work included the construction of a three-arched aqueduct over the Mells River, near Great Elm, called the Murtry Aqueduct. This construction, which can still be seen today, was never actually filled with water but boasts some decorative architectural features, including rusticated spandrels and plain pilasters between the arches. At the eastern end there is what was termed a skew arch, which is smaller than the three main arches.

Another larger aqueduct was also built at Springers Hill, Coleford, which similarly can still be seen today. A description of it on the South West Heritage Trust's website describes it as being made of coursed masonry blocks with furrowed dressings, with much of the ashlar having been robbed out – in other words, taken for reuse elsewhere. It contains two semicircular arches that are approximately 33 feet wide and slightly less in height. It is known locally as 'Huckyduck'.

Murtry Aqueduct, which was built to carry the Dorset and Somerset Canal over the Mells River, but because the canal was not completed it was never actually filled with water. (Photo courtesy of Derrick Hunt)

Coleford Aqueduct, built between 1800 and 1801 and known locally as 'Huckyduck'. (Photo courtesy of Derrick Hunt)

A more recent photograph of the north side of Coleford Aqueduct, which has two semicircular arches approximately 33 feet wide and slightly less in height. (Photo courtesy of Derrick Hunt)

Both the main line and the Somerset branch line of the canal would involve significant changes in water levels along their courses. The Act of Parliament had specified that conventional locks would be used on the main line and that caissons would be constructed on the branch, which dropped by 264 feet over its length. By August 1799, it was clear that the Robert Weldon design was unworkable and had been abandoned on the Somerset Coal Canal so something else would be needed. It was James Fussell himself, who was of course a knowledgeable ironworker, who came up with an alternative and proposed using vertical boat lifts.

Fussell called his design a balance lock and had it successfully patented in 1798, which was prior to the failure of Weldon's caisson locks, so it was something that he had evidently been working on in the background anyway. The balance lock was in fact very similar in principle to the boat lifts that James Green would design for the Grand Western Canal. Green's examples would become the first boat lifts to be commercially used anywhere in Great Britain.

The South West Heritage Trust's website gives a good description of how the lift operated, explaining that it consisted of a large masonry chamber divided into two sections.

> It had two tanks full of water, each being long enough to accommodate a barge. At the point where the canal changes height levels, they were arranged in a pit, side-by-side with one end towards the upper canal and one end towards the lower. Running the whole length of the space between the tanks was a central wall, on top of which were

A picture showing both lock chambers of James Fussell's trial balance lock, which were excavated by members of the Devon and Somerset Canal Study Group with the help of the Somersetshire Coal Canal Society in 2005 and 2006, with the kind permission of the landowner, Lord Oxford and Asquith of the Mells estate. (Photo courtesy of Derrick Hunt)

iron wheels. These were larger in diameter than the thickness of the central wall so that chains draped over them hung down slightly clear of the wall on each side. The tanks were suspended from the chains by a pulley arrangement and the lengths of the chains were such that when one tank was level with the bottom canal, the other was level with the top. The tank weights were adjusted to be equal, so that they were in balance and easy to move up and down with little effort. They could be moved with a hand crank geared to one of the wheels or by adding or removing a little water from one of the tanks.

The ends of the tanks could be clamped against the ends of the top and bottom canals to make a water tight seal. Doors or sliding panels were then removed to allow a boat to be floated from the canal into the tank. As the boat entered the tank a certain amount of water would have to flow out to make room for it – the weight of this water would be exactly the same as the weight of each boat with its cargo, so the balance of the tanks would not be upset. With the boats in the tanks, the doors or panels were replaced to seal the ends of the canals and the tanks. The tanks could then move up on one side and down on the other so as to deliver the boats to their new levels.

Fussell built the first of his lifts at Barrow Hill in 1800. It was designed to lift barges weighing up to 10 tons, 20 feet into the air. It was tested during September and October of that year and formally demonstrated on 13 October 1800. The *Bath Chronicle* carried a glowing report about it on 16 October that stated the lift had been operated several times

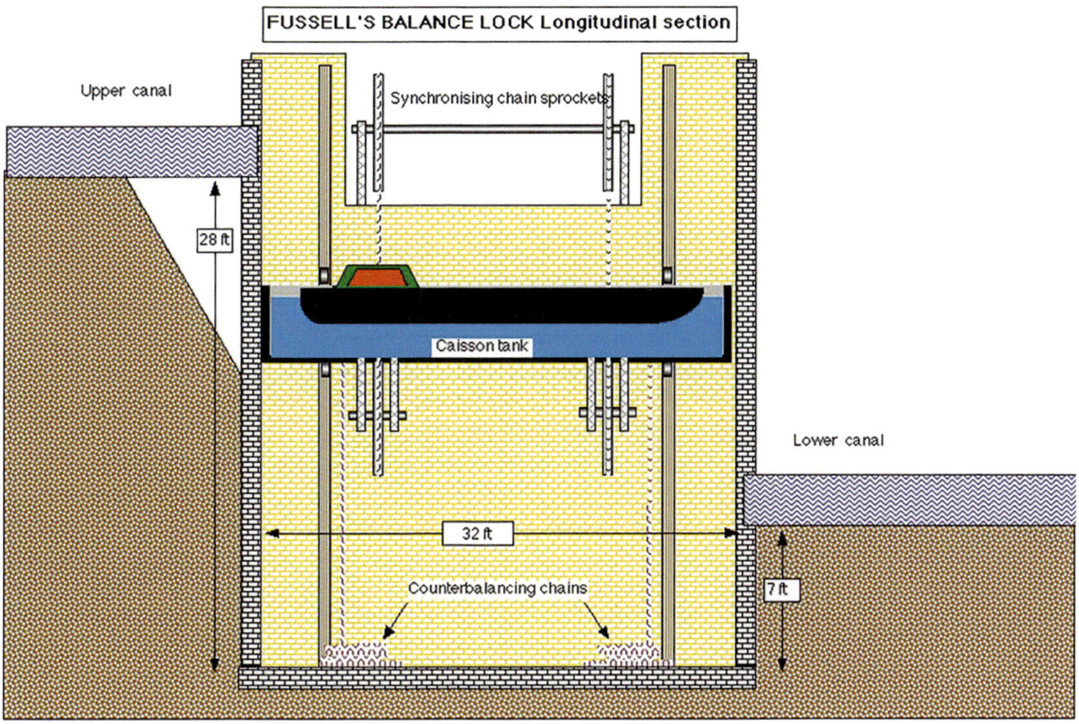

James Fussell's balance lock longitudinal section. (Photo courtesy of Derrick Hunt)

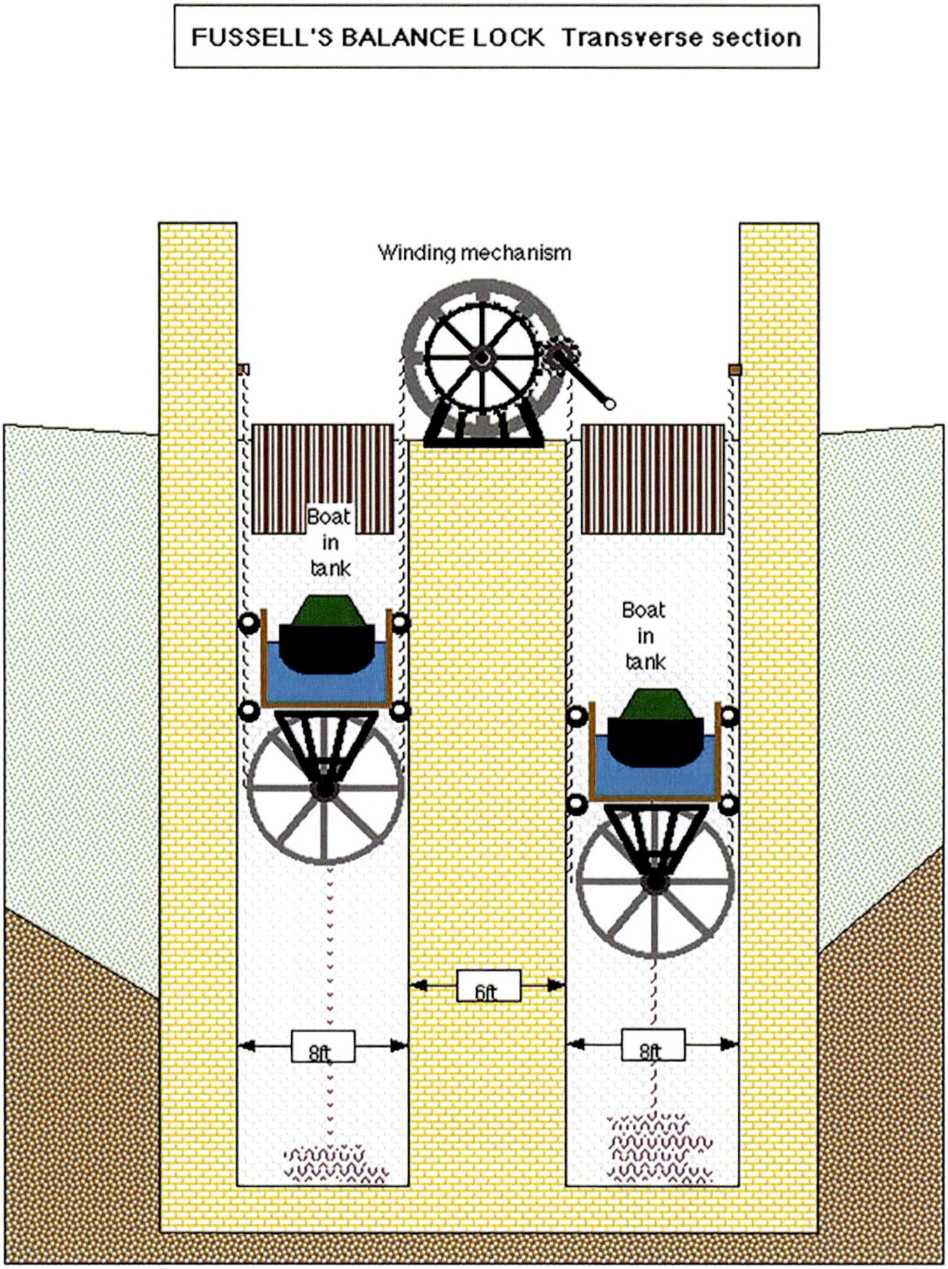

James Fussell's balance lock transverse section. (Photo courtesy of Derrick Hunt)

without any difficulty or problems and that engineers had inspected it carefully and declared themselves to be entirely satisfied with the results.

With the trials indicating that the balance locks did indeed work, Fussell and the company intended to build five more of them on the Barrow Hill section of the line, and pits for four of them were excavated. Frustratingly for him, though, and his iron mills, the canal company ran out of money in 1802 when there were less than 2 miles of the canal remaining to be excavated, leaving his boat lifts unfinished. Following excavations of the original balance lock in 2005 and 2006 by members of the Dorset and Somerset Canal Study Group and with the help of volunteers from the Somersetshire Coal Canal Society and the permission of the landowner, Lord Oxford and Asquith of the Mells estate, the structure was estimated at being 35 feet high and 30 feet long. The total width was around 24 feet, which included two pits and a central spine wall.

In an attempt to salvage the project, the company obtained a second Act of Parliament, the Dorset and Somerset Canal Act 1803, which would authorise them to raise more money and build railways along the route, instead of the canal, if that option would reduce the cost. Unfortunately, they were unable to raise any more finance and construction ceased in 1803 with the branch unfinished and the canal cancelled. Today you can still find tantalising glimpses of it in the North Somerset countryside, making it truly one of the lost wonders of the county's canal heyday.

Just south of Vobster Cross the road goes over the canal by this bridge, the arch of which has been filled in but the course of the canal bed can be made out on either side. In this picture Derrick Hunt of the Dorset and Somerset Canal Study Group is doing an inspection of the interior. (Photo courtesy of Derrick Hunt)

4

Bridgwater and Taunton Canal

The Bridgwater and Taunton Canal, which opened in 1827, came about as a knock-on effect of several schemes discussed during the eighteenth and nineteenth centuries to try and link the Bristol Channel to the English Channel, without having to sail around Cornwall. These discussions would more directly result in the construction of the Grand Western Canal, which we will describe in the next chapter. The Bridgwater and Taunton Canal would emerge from these various schemes as part of a breakaway plan ultimately intended to link Taunton to the port of Bristol.

Before the canal was built, it was possible to travel by boat between Taunton and Bridgwater by using the River Tone as far as Burrowbridge, where it joins the River Parrett just after Stanmoor Bridge. You could then take the Parrett for the final stage of the journey to Bridgwater. In order to be able to do this a group called the Conservators of the River Tone had made improvements to the river thanks to the Tone Navigation Acts of Parliament in 1699 and 1707. These Acts had given permission for the conservators to straighten and dredge the river and build the necessary infrastructure needed to manage its water levels.

The many schemes to establish a waterway between the two channels really began in 1768 when a committee of interested parties hired Shropshire engineer James Brindley to make a survey of a possible route. Similar to John Rennie, Brindley already had a wealth of experience in canal building. His suggested course between the Bristol and English Channels followed the River Tone for part of its route.

Over the next few years several more surveys were made, two of which eventually sought Parliamentary approval as the Grand Western Canal and the Bristol and Western Canal. Only the first of these was given the go-ahead, but because of the Napoleonic Wars construction was postponed. It was a time of national emergency, so defence projects became the priority in terms of both national and private finance.

Although work on the Grand Western Canal had been stopped for the time being, surveys of other routes continued. Then, in 1810, John Rennie was asked to look into the possibility of creating a ship canal between the River Parrett and Seaton in South Devon. The estimated cost of £1,000,000 made this economically unviable. As an alternative, he looked once again at the plans for the Bristol and Western Canal which had previously been submitted to Parliament. With some amendments, the plan was resubmitted and

Looking down the River Tone from Stanmoor Bridge towards Burrow Mump and its confluence with the River Parrett. This was part of the Tone Navigation prior to the building of the Bridgwater and Taunton Canal. (Photo © David Redwood)

finally authorised under the name of the Bristol and Taunton Canal by an Act of Parliament on 14 May 1811. This was the beginning of what would later become the Bridgwater and Taunton Canal.

The predicted cost of the canal was £429,990 and the Act gave the company powers to raise this through the sale of shares. Work began in 1822 with James Hollinsworth as the engineer and John Easton as senior surveyor. However, before long progress was impeded because an injunction had been brought against the company by one Revd Robert Gray as the construction was deviating from its authorised route. A further Act of Parliament, the Bristol and Taunton Canal Navigation Act of 1824, had to be passed before the company could follow their revised route. It was at this time that the name of the project was finally changed to the Bridgwater and Taunton Canal Company, with the link to Bristol abandoned. The predicted cost of what was now a much shorter canal was around £60,000.

The plan was to begin at Huntworth, a small hamlet to the south-east of Bridgwater, where the canal would join the River Parrett through a lock and a basin would be constructed to hold the barges. It would end at a place called Firepool Lock in Taunton, where it would join the River Tone. When completed this would make the canal around 12 miles in length. The ultimate aim being that once the Grand Western Canal was completed, from a link through the River Tone, there would be a continuous navigable watercourse all the way from the mouth of the River Parrett to the south coast through Exeter.

From the very start there was friction between the canal company and the conservators of the River Tone, who of course through their own Acts of Parliament oversaw the River Tone Navigation. The canal would create direct competition for the Tone Navigation, so the conservators were determined to safeguard their own interests. The conservators protested

A busy scene at Bridgwater Docks, *c.* 1900. (Photo courtesy of Bridgwater Heritage Group)

The Boat and Anchor Inn at Huntworth in 1977, close to where the Bridgwater and Taunton Canal joined the River Parrett when it first opened in 1827, via a basin and lock. (Photo courtesy of Railway and Canal Historical Society: Hugh Compton Collection)

that the canal company did not have the right to reach the Tone by going through the centre of Taunton, but in spite of these objections the canal company ploughed ahead and the connection between canal and river was finally opened on 3 January 1827.

During the early years of the canal's existence animosity continued between the two parties until eventually they jointly proposed a new Act of Parliament to authorise the sale of the Tone Navigation to the canal company. This was obtained in July 1832 and required the canal company to erect a new iron bridge to replace the existing North Town Bridge, as this hampered access to the wharves in Taunton. They also had the power to construct a lock and a short length of canal at French Weir to connect with the Grand Western Canal. As a provision of this Act, the conservators could conduct an annual inspection of the canal and if it was not being maintained in good order, they would have the power to resume their ownership of the river navigation.

There was also competition at the Bridgwater end when, in 1836, the Bristol and Exeter Railway obtained their own Act of Parliament giving them permission to build a line through Bridgwater. Because of this the canal company decided to move the starting point of the canal to a floating harbour at Bridgwater Docks, now the site of Bridgwater Marina, from where it would then join the river. This would make it around 14 miles in length. The Huntworth link and basin were subsequently closed and filled in. In order to do this a further Act of Parliament was obtained on 21 April 1837.

This new work, which was completed in 1841, included the creation of an inner basin covering 4 acres and a smaller outer basin of around ½ an acre. The two basins were connected to one another by a lock and to the river by a ship lock, which consisted of a

Firepool Lock in Taunton, where the Bridgwater and Taunton Canal joins the River Tone. (Photo courtesy of Railway and Canal Historical Society: Hugh Compton Collection)

single 40-foot gate and a barge lock with a pair of 14-foot gates. A bascule bridge carried a road over the barge lock, which worked on the same principal as the later Tower Bridge in London but was manually operated. It was originally made of cast iron, although following refurbishment in 1981 it was replaced by a steel replica. The whole outer basin could be used as a lock by larger ships of up to 600 tons. The estimated cost of £25,000 for the scheme escalated to nearly £100,000, most of which was raised by mortgage.

After the opening of the floating harbour in Bridgwater trade increased from around 90,000 tons a year to 120,000 tons, with an estimated 2,400 vessels using the docks annually. As with many canal systems, coal and stone transporters were by far the biggest users.

As well as the locks at either end of the canal there were a further four locks along its main waterway, all of which can still be seen today. These are Maunsel Top or Higher Lock (No. 2), Maunsel Bottom or Lower Lock (No. 3), Kings Lock (No. 4) and Standards Lock (No. 5). Firepool Lock in Taunton was lock No. 1. The work also included the construction of eleven brick bridges needed to carry roads over the water and more than twelve timber swing bridges to enable farmers whose land had been dissected by the system to cross from one side to the other.

Apparently, the operating system employed at Maunsel was unique to the Bridgwater and Taunton Canal. It was called paddle gearing and used metal ball weights at the top and metal cylinder weights at the bottom.

Although the canal was proving to be very successful, it was far from being profitable as it was being crippled by the interest payments on the mortgage. It was hoped that the opening of the Grand Western Canal in 1838 and the Chard Canal in 1842 would increase

Bridgwater Docks tidal basin in 1972, in the foreground is the upper gate of the barge lock. (Photo courtesy of Railway and Canal Historical Society: Hugh Compton Collection)

The bascule bridge over the barge lock at Bridgwater Docks seen in operation in 1910. (Photo courtesy of Bridgwater Heritage Group)

The operating system at Maunsel Lock with its unique paddle gearing, pictured in 2008. (Photo courtesy of Railway and Canal Historical Society: Peter Brown Collection)

traffic and revenue, but their impact was very low. By the 1850s, due to competition from the railways, trade had collapsed and the company found itself in the hands of the receivers.

However, salvation was to come from an unlikely source as the Bristol and Exeter Railway bought both the canal and the docks for £64,000 after obtaining an Act of Parliament to do so in 1866. The railway company considered the canal to be a useful partner to their existing business because of the large quantities of coal it brought to the floating harbour, which of course for a steam-reliant operation like theirs was a necessity. Because of this the canal was kept open and in good condition and the conservators of the River Tone were allowed to continue making periodic inspections and reporting any issues directly to them.

The main problem created by this partnership was that the canal and railway each needed water but there simply wasn't enough to accommodate the needs of both. The canal's main source was supplied via the Charlton Pumping Station at Creech, where water was pumped into it from the River Tone. At this point the two waterways were only around 300 yards apart. Then once every fortnight large amounts of water were discharged from the canal when the floating harbour in Bridgwater was quite literally flushed through in an attempt to stop silt building up. At the same time the railway company was extracting water to supply its station and steam locomotive sheds in Taunton. The result was that at times water got too low and the canal started to clog up with weeds.

In the end the railway company decided to transfer most of the cargo carried by barges onto its trucks, and in so doing allowed the canal to spiral into decline. Things got even worse in 1877 when the Bristol & Exeter Railway merged with the Great Western Railway and the new management prioritised supplying the railway with water, leaving the canal to continue deteriorating. By 1907 all commercial traffic had stopped on the canal and it was effectively closed.

During the Second World War, similar to the Kennet and Avon Canal, the Bridgwater and Taunton Canal was used as part of Britain's defence against a possible invasion from Nazi Germany. It became part of the Taunton Stop Line, a continuous defensive line running along rivers, railway embankments and canals all the way from Seaton on the south coast to the mouth of the River Parrett in Bridgwater Bay. Bunkers and anti-tank obstacles were positioned all along the banks, many of which can still be visited today, and swing bridges were removed and replaced with fixed timber bridges.

Charlton Pumping Station at Creech St Michael in 2000. It pumped water into the canal from the River Tone. (Photo courtesy of Railway and Canal Historical Society: Peter Brown Collection)

The dredger *Bertha*, a steam-powered boat built in 1844 to remove silt from Bridgwater Docks, in 1972. (Photo courtesy of Bridgwater Heritage Group)

In 1947, although now unused, the canal passed into public ownership under the Transport Act of that year. Then, in the early 1950s, the Inland Waterways Association began to take an interest in restoring the canal as a leisure facility, although the British Transport Commission were against the idea and padlocked all the lock gates to make sure nobody could use them. What they were interested in was the commercial transport of water, which from 1962 onwards was pumped from the canal to Durleigh Reservoir in order to provide water for the British Cellophane factory in Bridgwater.

In 1963, the canal fell under the jurisdiction of the British Waterways Board, which of course was established as a result of the Transport Act of 1962 to take control of inland waterways. Then, with the passing of the Transport Act 1968, the canal was classified as a 'remainder waterway', which meant it was to be maintained to the minimum level possible consistent only with public safety. Soon afterwards, part of a wall that took the canal between West Street and Albert Street in Bridgwater collapsed and although the bed of the canal was cleared to ensure water could reach the dock, the towpath itself would remain blocked for another nine years. Bridgwater Docks finally closed to all shipping in 1971 and the British Waterways Board ceased maintaining the canal for navigation from that time onwards.

In the late 1960s, the Inland Waterways Association continued to promote redevelopment of the canal, producing a report that suggested it had the potential for use as a linear country park. This was followed by a second report made by the County Planning Officer for Somerset County Council after which funds were made available for maintenance and restoration work. The Countryside Act of 1968 provided a framework for such action.

By 1974, with funding from Somerset County Council, the British Waterways Board had refurbished both of the Maunsel Locks and there was money set aside for maintaining the towpath. Then, in December of that year, the council purchased Bridgwater Docks from its then owners, British Railways. By 1980, the restoration had included Kings Lock and Standards Lock, as well as the bottom gates of Newtown Lock, where the canal enters the docks. Other work included raising the height of some bridges, rebuilding several swing bridges and renovating the cutting in Bridgwater between West Street and Albert Street.

The cutting that took the canal between West Street and Albert Street in Bridgwater, pictured in the early 1970s after part of the wall collapsed, debris from which can be seen in the distance between the two arches. (Photo courtesy of Railway and Canal Historical Society: Hugh Compton Collection)

Another picture of the Bridgwater cutting from the early 1970s, this time showing both the collapsed wall and the blocked towpath. (Photo courtesy of Railway and Canal Historical Society: Hugh Compton Collection)

By 1984, a six-year plan to restore the canal had been fully costed and agreed by all interested parties, notably the British Waterways Board, Somerset County Council, Sedgemoor District Council and Taunton Deane Borough Council. The West Country branch of the Inland Waterways Association offered the services of their Waterway Recovery Group and, with everyone pulling together, the canal finally reopened in 1994.

Although boating is now permitted on the canal, there is no longer a navigable connection to the River Parrett at its northern end. This is because the river is tidal and contains salt water, whereas the freshwater canal is still used as a source of drinking water for the people of Bridgwater. The docks themselves have been regenerated and although several listed buildings associated with the canal survive, there are also new apartments around what is now the marina, notably occupying an old warehouse built in the 1840s.

Another attraction along the towpath is an installation called the Somerset Space Walk, a scale model of the solar system, the scale being 530,000,000 to 1. It includes a model globe representing the sun positioned at Maunsel, where you can also find a canal visitor centre. The various planets are located along the towpath in both directions at carefully worked out intervals. The whole thing was designed by local man Pip Youngman. From Maunsel, the trail can be walked in both directions, ending at either the Brewhouse Theatre in Taunton or Morrison's supermarket in Bridgwater. Each of these locations marks the position of Pluto, nearly 7 miles away.

Today the Bridgwater and Taunton Canal is owned by the Canal and River Trust, while Bridgwater Docks are still owned by Somerset County Council and leased to the Canal River Trust.

Maunsel Lock in 1990. (Photo courtesy of Railway and Canal Historical Society: Peter Brown Collection)

An old postcard depicting Newtown Lock. (Photo courtesy of Railway and Canal Historical Society: Hugh Compton Collection)

Another historic view of Bridgwater Docks, with the canal entrance to the left of the buildings. Today the docks are owned by Somerset County Council. (Photo courtesy of Bridgwater Heritage Group)

5

Grand Western Canal

Similar to both the Bridgwater and Taunton Canal and the Dorset and Somerset Canal, the Grand Western Canal, which would run between Taunton and Tiverton in Devon, came about as a consequence of various schemes designed to create an overland waterway between the Bristol Channel and the English Channel, avoiding the many dangers associated with a seaborne passage between the two. Another purpose of this particular stretch of the canal was to supply limestone and coal to limekilns along the route, where quicklime was created for use as a fertiliser in West Country agriculture and in the building sector.

Once given Parliamentary approval, the canal was built in two phases. The first section, from Lowdwells on the Somerset–Devon border to Tiverton, was opened in 1814. It was capable of accommodating broad-beam barges that could transport up to 40 tons each. The Somerset section, of which we are more concerned, was suitable for using tub boats – smaller craft that could transport 8 tons each. This section opened in 1839 and would include an inclined plane and seven boat lifts, which were the earliest to see commercial service in Great Britain. Much of the Devon section remains in water to this day and is now a designated country park, while the Somerset section has almost entirely disappeared from view.

Limekilns at Tiverton Basin, 1975. (Photo courtesy of Railway and Canal Historical Society: Hugh Compton Collection)

In 1768, the notable engineer James Brindley was commissioned by a committee to look into the route of a canal that would link the two channels. Brindley had actually worked on the Bridgewater Canal between Worsley and Runcorn in north-west England, which opened in 1761 and was regarded as the first great achievement of the golden age of canals. It is interesting to note that this was thirty years prior to John Rennie's first foray into the canal world, his earliest project being the Stowmarket Navigation in 1791.

Brindley duly appointed Robert Whitworth to complete the study in 1769. This project was labelled the Exeter to Uphill Canal and it traced a course that would run from the River Exe, either from Exeter or Topsham, to Taunton. From Taunton, it would follow the existing River Tone Navigation as far as Burrowbridge. From here, it would involve digging a second canal that would meander towards Glastonbury, Wells and Axbridge, before emerging on the North Somerset coast at Uphill to the south of Weston-super-Mare, from where it was a short trip up the coast to the port of Bristol. At the time nothing came of this, but almost thirty years later in the 1790s a new committee was formed – the Grand Western Canal Committee – with a view to revisiting the scheme.

In 1794, John Rennie was approached to make another assessment of the route between north and south coasts. His intended route would begin at Topsham on the River Exe to the south of Exeter, which caused some opposition from the authorities in the city. The reason for this being that a ship canal had already been built in the 1560s that went from the River Exe opposite Topsham to a quay in Exeter. By directing the new canal towards Topsham itself and avoiding Exeter, it meant the new canal company would not have to pay to use the ship canal in order to transport goods, particularly coal, which of course would deny the ship canal owners a valuable source of income.

Aqueduct that once carried the Grand Western Canal across the carriage drive that led to Nynehead Court. Reproduced from a postcard postmarked 1906. (Author's collection)

The aqueduct over the former drive to Nynehead Court, pictured in August 1976. (Photo courtesy of Railway and Canal Historical Society: Hugh Compton Collection)

In spite of objections, the plan was submitted to Parliament and the Grand Western Canal Act was passed on 24 March 1796. The Act authorised the construction of a canal between Taunton and Topsham with branches to Tiverton and Cullompton. The required water supply would be provided by building three reservoirs along the route, one near the River Tone and two near the River Culm. Other water could be derived from any other available sources within 2,000 yards of the waterway. From Taunton, the plan would be to use the existing River Tone Navigation and the River Parrett for onward transportation. Bear in mind that the Bridgwater and Taunton Canal did not exist yet, so would not have entered into the equation. However, construction of the canal appears to have been delayed, probably because of political unrest in France ultimately leading to the Napoleonic Wars which would have an effect on the finances of potential investors.

Fourteen years later, in 1810, work finally began on the first section of the canal under the direction of one John Thomas. Construction began in the middle with the section between Lowdwells to Tiverton. The reason for this being that there was a large potential trade in limestone between quarries at Canonsleigh and Tiverton which would generate income immediately.

Thanks to John Rennie's surveying and engineering skills and in spite of the undulating terrain the canal crossed, the water level on this 11¼-mile section remained constant all along its course, with no requirement to build any locks or boat lifts. Achieving this remarkable feat greatly increased the number of earthworks required and a further Act of Parliament, the Grand Western Canal Act 1811, had to be obtained before this could proceed. Costs were also rising and in 1812 a third Act of Parliament was passed in order to authorise increased charges for carriage of goods along the system. Eventually the work on this section was completed at the cost of £244,500 and on 25 August 1814 the first vessel travelled from Lowdwells to Tiverton carrying a shipment of coal.

Although the first section of the canal was now open, it would be another seventeen years before work would commence on the next part of the project. It seems that following the completion of the Tiverton to Lowdwells stage, traffic using it was far less than

Lowdwells Lock, on the Somerset–Devon border, pictured in May 2008. (Photo courtesy of Railway and Canal Historical Society: Peter Brown Collection)

expected so the money it generated was negligible. The only profitable area for the canal company was in supplying the limekilns. Interest, therefore, in continuing the canal either south towards the Exe or north towards Taunton evaporated.

The situation changed in 1827 with the opening of the Bridgwater and Taunton Canal, which would now make onward navigation to the mouth of the River Parrett and Bristol more accessible if a link between the two canals was made. With this in mind, in 1830 James Green, who had been the architect of the Bude Canal in Cornwall, was asked to submit a survey of the 13-mile extension from Lowdwells to Taunton. His proposal, which was accepted by the committee, was to build a tub boat canal using a revolutionary system of vertical lifts, which would raise boats between water levels instead of using conventional locks. He would incorporate an inclined plane and seven of these boat lifts to cope with the 270-foot change in levels, all at an estimated cost of £65,000.

Tub boats were smaller than the barges used on the Tiverton section, although they still needed to be pulled along by horse. In fact, several tub boats could be linked together like a train and pulled along by just one animal. However, because of their size it would mean a transferral of cargos at the lock at Lowdwells before they could continue their journey to Taunton. There was no standardisation of tub boat sizes, but they were generally between 20 feet and 26 feet in length and 6 feet 6 inches wide. Because of their size they were also very flexible and could be transferred easily between parts of canals that were in water and the out of water inclines, where they could be raised onto carts.

The original Grand Western Canal Act of 1796 had envisaged the canal joining the River Tone at Taunton, but as we saw in the last chapter there had been disputes between the Bridgwater and Taunton Canal Company and the conservators of the River Tone which

Aqueduct built in 1828 to carry the Grand Western Canal over the River Tone near Nynehead, photographed in 1976. (Photo courtesy of Railway and Canal Historical Society: Hugh Compton Collection)

This picture of the Tone Aqueduct, also from 1976, shows the cast-iron trough through which the barges traversed. (Photo courtesy of Railway and Canal Historical Society: Hugh Compton Collection)

Old postcard of the French Weir in Taunton where a link was built between the Grand Western Canal and the River Tone in 1834. (Photo courtesy of Railway and Canal Historical Society: Hugh Compton Collection)

made life difficult for all concerned. On contemplation, the committee of the Grand Western Canal decided that it would be better if they could avoid joining the River Tone and instead make a direct link into the Bridgwater and Taunton Canal. In order to do this, they successfully purchased the land required. As a result, a new Act of Parliament, the Bridgwater and Taunton Canal Navigation Act 1832, was obtained, which required the Bridgwater and Taunton Canal to build a link between the River Tone and the Grand Western Canal. This was built in 1834, leaving the river below French Weir and heading north-west to Frieze Hill, where there was a right-angled connection to the line of the canal.

Work on the section finally kicked off in 1831 and within a short period of time bridges had been constructed across the intended course of the waterway at both Bradford-on-Tone and near Langford Budville, the latter being called Harpford Bridge. The first boat lift was built at Nynehead, along with two aqueducts. Six more boat lifts would quickly follow at Greenham, Winsbeer, Terfusis, Allerford, Norton Fitzwarren and Taunton, but there were teething problems with the design which was to cause a delay in the opening of the canal. There were also issues with the inclined plane and although the canal partially opened as far as Wellington in 1835, in January 1836 James Green was sacked by the canal company and William Alexander Provis, another renowned canal engineer, was asked to survey the work so far and assess the problems facing both the lifts and the inclined plane.

With regards to the boat lifts, the idea was certainly not a new one, but where it had been experimented with elsewhere problems had always seemed to follow. As we have already seen, in 1798 Robert Weldon had tried to build something similar at Combe Hay on the Somerset Coal Canal with mixed results, which ended in them being replaced by conventional locks. We also noted how James Fussell had built a type of lift on the Dorset and Somerset Canal in 1800, but the project was abandoned before completion. There were other examples as well, but they always seem to have fallen short of what was required. Most, if not all, of these had been inspired by the theories of Dr James Anderson from Edinburgh, who had proposed the principal in around 1796.

Perhaps it was a bit cavalier on the part of James Green to go ahead and build all seven of the planned lifts without having first tried a working prototype that he knew would be successful. In his design, two caissons were suspended from three carrying wheels by wrought-iron chains. Each of the wheels measured 16 feet in diameter. Tub boats would be floated into each caisson which would then be sealed. They worked on a balance system whereby the descending caisson provided sufficient force to raise the identical ascending caisson. This was achieved by adding extra water to the upper caisson.

In assessing the problems with the lifts, William Provis discovered that Green had not followed Anderson's suggestions to the letter. He noted that the water in the caisson chambers should have been at a lower level than that in the canal. As this had not been done, the lower caisson could not sink deep enough for either boat to be floated out of their respective caissons. In order to rectify it, lock chambers had to be constructed at the base of each lift. When these were filled with water from the upper level, it enabled the boats to disgorge from their caissons and float out into the canal. Once corrected, it took the boats roughly eight-and-a-half minutes to pass through the system. However the last lift to be built, which was at Greenham, had adhered to Anderson's principles and enabled boats to pass through in just three minutes.

Nynehead Lift, April 2000. (Photo courtesy of Railway and Canal Historical Society: Peter Brown Collection)

As for the incline, this was at Wellisford. It was a double-tracked railway that had a vertical height of 81 feet and a length of 440 feet. On each track ran a wheeled cradle that was big enough to carry one of the tub boats. The system on the incline was powered by water – a 10-ton tank of water was suspended in each of two wells. Water would be added to the uppermost tank until its weight exceeded that of the other tank, the cradle and the boat combined, causing it to descend and so raise the cradle. At the bottom, a valve would release the water from the tank. Green had built something very similar on the Bude Canal, where, in his defence, it had worked. At Wellisford, however, it didn't seem to work because the tanks were much too small. On the Bude Canal, a tank holding 15 tons of water was required to raise a boat weighing 6 tons. The Grand Western Canal used tub boats generally weighing 8 tons, but the tanks only held 10 tons of water, whereas tests indicated that about 25 tons were needed. Provis solved the issue by installing a steam engine to provide the power instead.

Once Provis had finished his investigations and his suggested remedial work had been carried out, the extension between Lowdwells and Taunton was fully opened on 28 June 1838. The final cost of this section of the canal is thought to have been in the region of £80,000. Income from tolls collected on the canal between 1838 and 1844 raised from £2,754 to £4,926. However, as with all the examples we have studied, a common competitor for the canal's business was about to threaten its existence.

A different view of the Nynehead Lift, this time pictured in 1976. (Photo courtesy of Railway and Canal Historical Society: Hugh Compton Collection)

The track of the Wellisford Incline, pictured in 1976. (Photo courtesy of Railway and Canal Historical Society: Hugh Compton Collection)

The Bristol & Exeter Railway reached Taunton in 1842 and Exeter in 1844, with a branch to Tiverton opening in 1848. It wasn't long before the canal's customers and income had all but disappeared, and by 1853 its income no longer met its operational costs. In 1864, an Act of Parliament was obtained to sell the canal to the railway company and abandon the Somerset stretch entirely. The transfer took place on 13 April 1865, with the tub boat section closing in 1867. All of the boat lifts were dismantled and most of the route was sold back to the original landowners.

The Somerset section of the Grand Western Canal is now almost completely drained of water and gradually disappearing into the landscape. On the plus side, a public footpath has been established along much of its route for people to follow. The only boat lift that still has substantial remains is the one at Nynehead, where archaeological excavations were carried out between 1998 and 2003 by the Somerset Industrial Archaeological Society, and you will now find an information board at the site.

In 2017, the Friends of the Grand Western Canal announced a scheme to rebuild around 2 miles of canal to the west of Taunton. They also plan to build a working replica of one of James Green's boat lifts near the Silk Mills car park, with a new section of canal built across empty public land to join the River Tone below French Weir. This would roughly follow the link constructed by the Bridgwater and Taunton Canal in 1834. Around ½ a mile

The site of the Allerford boat lift in 1976. (Photo courtesy of Railway and Canal Historical Society: Hugh Compton Collection)

Remains of the engine house at the Wellisford Incline in 1976. (Photo courtesy of Railway and Canal Historical Society: Hugh Compton Collection)

of the original canal would also be restored to provide moorings for boats to use the lift. The scheme is supported by Taunton Council and many local dignitaries.

The Devon section of the Grand Western Canal is now owned and run by Devon County Council as an 11-mile-long linear country park and local nature reserve. Locals call it the Tiverton Canal and here you will now find the Tiverton Canal Company, a truly unique living heritage attraction, where staff dressed in clothing of a bygone era will take you on a relaxing and magical ride on one of the very last remaining horse-drawn passenger barges in Great Britain.

Today you can still take a horse-drawn boat trip on the Grand Western Canal from Tiverton Basin. This picture from August 1987 shows a trip on the *Tivertonian.* (Photo courtesy of Railway and Canal Historical Society: Peter Brown Collection)

6

Chard Canal

Chard was a mill town at the very heart of the Industrial Revolution in Somerset and its skyline is still dotted with mill buildings from the early nineteenth century, a reminder of its past as a centre for the lace-making industry. By the early 1800s the expanding town had an increasing need for a cheaper method of transport to bring coal and building materials to the town and to take the woollen and lace textiles it made to markets elsewhere. It was therefore an ideal place to be connected to a canal network with all the advantages that this would offer.

After featuring in the dialogues of several proposals that didn't materialise, it would eventually be visited by its own tub boat canal, which ran from the town to a junction with the Bridgwater and Taunton Canal at Creech St Michael. It was completed in 1842 but was never commercially profitable, so closed in 1868. However, many of its main engineering features are still clearly visible in the landscape.

Long before the Chard Canal was even considered there had been several plans put forward to build a ship canal that would quite literally take large vessels of up to 200 tons right across Somerset and Devon, from the Bristol Channel to the English Channel. Chard first featured in a route surveyed by Robert Whitworth in 1769, which would run from the mouth of the River Parrett to Seaton in South Devon. Further schemes were promoted in 1793, 1810 and 1825, generally given the working title of the English and Bristol Channels Canal. The exact routes of these surveys varied but all started around Seaton and would take in the valleys of the rivers Axe, Isle, Tone or Parrett. They would also all cross the Blackdown Hills via Chard.

Taking a canal through Chard was never going to be an easy task as it is located high on a ridge; in fact, at 500 feet above sea level it is actually the highest town in Somerset. The town has a very unusual feature, a stream running along either side of Fore Street. One of the streams eventually flows north into the Bristol Channel and the other reaches the English Channel to the south. This would obviously imply that if a canal was built here, the water would have to flow downhill from it in both directions, north and south.

The 1810 survey was made by John Rennie, who advocated a smaller ship canal suitable for vessels of up to 120 tons, but the estimated cost of £1,330,000 made it unviable. The 1825 survey was carried out by the great Thomas Telford, one of the most significant civil

Tollhouse at the junction between the Chard Canal and the Bridgwater and Taunton Canal at Creech St Michael in 1972. (Photo courtesy of Railway and Canal Historical Society: Philip and Rodney Weaver Collection)

engineers to have worked during the Industrial Revolution in Great Britain. He envisaged a system capable of taking vessels of 200 tons with a draught of 15 feet. His scheme would involve thirty locks and would run from Stolford on the Bristol Channel to Beer in Devon, passing through Creech St Michael, Ilminster and Chard along the way. Although the cost of this was estimated at £1,700,000, the scheme was eventually adopted and proposed to Parliament. The English and Bristol Channels Ship Canal Act 1825 was subsequently passed on 6 July 1825. The canal company that was formed to promote this scheme managed to raise over £1,500,000 in subscriptions, but for whatever reason no further action was taken, the canal was never built, and the company was wound up in 1828.

However, when the Bridgwater and Taunton Canal opened in 1827, this brought about interest in linking Chard to this new waterway and ultimately to the Bristol Channel. James Green, who of course was working on the Grand Western Canal at the time, was asked to survey a route in 1831. The route he suggested would join the Bridgwater and Taunton Canal at Creech St Michael and would be 13½ miles in length. Because Chard was around 231 feet higher than the canal at Creech, his project would need to include two boat lifts, two tunnels and two inclined planes at points along its course. The estimated cost of all of this was £57,000.

An Act of Parliament – the Chard Canal Act 1834 – was obtained in June of that year, authorising the raising of the £57,000, with an additional £20,000 if required. However, when it came to actually raising the money there seemed to be little interest among the business fraternity of Chard itself, who had only recently had their fingers burnt thanks to

Sign for the Canal Inn at Wrantage as it appeared in 1972, close to the Chard Canal. (Photo courtesy of Railway and Canal Historical Society: Philip and Rodney Weaver Collection)

the 1825 ship canal fiasco. That said, the capital required was duly raised but most of it was provided by just five individuals, all of whom were wealthy businessmen from Bristol who were also heavily involved with the Bridgwater and Taunton Canal. The five in question were Isaac Cooke, John and William Cave, Joseph Cookson and Joseph Reynolds. In fact, only £3,250 of the first subscription of £46,850 came from the people of Chard.

Work on the canal began at Wrantage in June 1835, with Sydney Hall appointed as its engineer, replacing James Green, who the following year would also be unceremoniously sacked by the Grand Western Canal Company. Taking into consideration the problems that Green had experienced with his boat lifts on the Grand Western Canal, Hall decided to write these out of the Chard plan and replace them with two further inclined planes. Remarkably for such a huge responsibility, Hall was only twenty-one years old at the time.

Sydney Hall also felt it was imperative to make a series of other changes to Green's original plan, including the construction of another tunnel above one of the inclines. This would enable the line of the canal to be built at a lower level. He also added a conventional lock to be positioned at a point where there was a 7-foot change in water levels. Finally, the length of the Chard incline was also to be increased.

The Chard Canal at Wrantage in 1975. (Photo courtesy of Railway and Canal Historical Society: Hugh Compton Collection)

Remains of an embankment between the Bridgwater and Taunton Canal junction with the Chard Canal and the River Tone Aqueduct, May 1999. (Photo courtesy of Railway and Canal Historical Society: Hugh Compton Collection)

All of this new planning meant that the construction costs spiralled from what had originally been quoted. Because of this a new Act of Parliament, the Chard Canal Company Act 1840, had to be passed in March 1840. This revised Act authorised the company to raise another £80,000 and obtain a mortgage of £26,000. Even with all of this implemented, progress on the canal was much slower than expected and a third Act, the Chard Canal Act 1841, allowed construction to continue beyond the original seven-year timeframe given for the project.

The canal was opened in stages rather than on one grand occasion, with the first stage from Creech St Michael to Ilminster opening on 15 May 1841, followed by the stretch to Dowlish Ford on 3 February 1842. After a number of delays elsewhere, particularly at Wrantage where a rope broke on the incline causing damage to the infrastructure, the work was finally completed on 24 May 1842. The original estimate of the cost of construction was of course £57,000, but the actual cost was nearer £140,000.

After all the delays and changes that were made, the finished canal was 13½ miles long and had five sections at different levels, which were linked by the four inclined planes at Chard Common (86 feet), Ilminster (82 feet), Wrantage (27 feet) and Thornfalcon (28 feet). There was one lock at Dowlish Ford, four aqueducts and three tunnels. The tunnels were located at Herne Hill (300 yards long), Crimson Hill (2,000 yards long) and Lillesdon (200 yards long). The original proposal was to dig a deep cutting across one side of Herne Hill, with an aqueduct over the Chard to Ilminster turnpike road, but this was later changed to a tunnel.

Remains of a demolished aqueduct on the Chard Canal at Wrantage. (Photo courtesy of Railway and Canal Historical Society: Hugh Compton Collection)

Aqueduct taking the Chard Canal across the River Tone at Creech St Michael. (Photo courtesy of Railway and Canal Historical Society: Hugh Compton Collection)

North portal of the Crimson Hill Tunnel near Wrantage in 1987. (Photo courtesy of Railway and Canal Historical Society: Stanley Holland Collection)

Most of the canal that was in water was 23 feet wide and 3 feet deep, but in some places it narrowed to around 12 feet. The canal was operated with horse-drawn tub boats that were about 26 feet long and 6½ feet wide.

The inclines at Thornfalcon, Wrantage and Ilminster were all double-acting. They were built using two parallel tracks, each containing a six-wheeled caisson. The caisson would be filled with water and the boat floated into it. Once sealed the caisson would be pulled onto the rails of the incline for its downhill or uphill journey. The two caissons were linked together by a chain which passed around a horizontal drum situated at the top of the incline. Power for the movement of the caissons was provided by over-filling the top one, with the extra weight causing it to descend and the other to rise. During the operation of the caissons, more water would obviously pass down each incline, rather than up them. So, in order to provide the necessary amount of water required near the start of the line, a new reservoir was built to the north-east of Chard on the River Isle.

The incline at Chard Common was the exception and consisted of a single track, with the tub boats being carried on a four-wheeled cradle 86 feet up or down the slope. The cradle was attached to a rope powered by a water turbine manufactured by Whitelaw and Stirrat, which ran at a speed of 60–63 rpm and used 725 cubic feet of water per minute.

As for the three tunnels, the one at Herne Hill was 14 feet wide, which made it just wide enough to allow boats travelling in opposite directions to pass through it. However, the examples at Lillesdon and Crimson Hill were only wide enough to accommodate one boat. Having said that, the Crimson Hill Tunnel included a double width passing area, which was roughly halfway through its course. This allowed the passing of boats from both directions simultaneously.

At the Chard end of the canal the terminus was at a place called Chard Basin, where wharves and warehousing were built. This was later the site of a flour mill, B. G. Wyatt Ltd, which was close to the now closed but once very popular Furnham Inn in Furnham Road. All the old buildings have since vanished, the site infilled and built over with modern housing.

Once the canal was officially open there was an immediate benefit to the people of Chard as coal prices fell. Coal from South Wales carried by the Chard Canal was taken by road to local villages and to towns as far away as Lyme Regis and Sidmouth on the south coast. However, for the canal company itself, the opening of the scheme pretty much coincided with its quick decline. Construction costs were of course much higher than anticipated and the income the canal generated was never more than a third of what had been projected, so they were never able to even meet the interest payments on their debts.

The main freight carried on the canal was stone and coal. In its first three years the annual tonnage rose from 25,835 tons to 33,284 tons. However, the age of the railways had already arrived and competition was fierce. The amount of goods carried on the canal soon began to decrease. In an attempt to salvage something from the project, the canal company submitted a proposal through Parliament to convert the canal into a railway, which led to the passing of the Chard Railway Act 1847. The name of the company thereafter changed to the Chard Railway, but it was never a realistic proposition as the company was struggling to repay its debts, let alone finance a radical transition. In the end the canal went into receivership in 1853.

Accommodation Aqueduct on the embankment between the Tone and Ruishton aqueducts at Creech St Michael, photographed in 1972. (Photo courtesy of Railway and Canal Historical Society: Philip and Rodney Weaver Collection)

As we have already seen, the Bristol & Exeter Railway had previously purchased two other struggling canals, the Grand Western Canal in 1864 and the Bridgwater and Taunton Canal in 1866. This was partially done to stop rival railway companies obtaining them, particularly the London & South Western Railway. In 1867, they decided to purchase the Chard Canal as well, paying £5,945, with the takeover and closing of the canal being authorised by the Bristol & Exeter Railway Act of 1867. The following year the receivers were discharged and the canal was finally closed as a working waterway.

There are still many reminders of this short-lived episode in local history along its now-vanished course. Chard Reservoir, for instance, which was the main water supplier for the canal and later owned by Lord Poulett, was bought by South Somerset District Council in 1990 and transformed into a designated nature reserve. Surrounded by woodland, it is said to provide a habitat for over 150 species of birds.

The footprints of all four of the inclined planes have also all survived, as well as the three tunnels. A bridge on the Thornfalcon to Creech road near Lower Farm is now a Grade II-listed structure, and the three-arched aqueduct which carried the canal over the River Tone is largely intact, although it no longer has its parapets. You will also encounter the odd pillbox at intervals as part of the Taunton Stop Line ran along the canal during the Second World War. Here and there you may still encounter stretches that are still in water, giving you a clearer view of how this incredible piece of innovation would have looked in its brief heyday.

Site of the B. G. Wyatt Ltd flour mill at Chard Basin in 1973. (Photo courtesy of Railway and Canal Historical Society: Philip and Rodney Weaver Collection)

Chard Reservoir in 1972, created to supply water for Chard Canal. (Photo courtesy of Railway and Canal Historical Society: Philip and Rodney Weaver Collection)

The embankment of Chard Canal at Wrantage in 1976, surmounted by a Second World War pillbox. The canal formed part of the Taunton Stop Line. (Photo courtesy of Railway and Canal Historical Society: Hugh Compton Collection)

7

Ivel and Parrett Navigations

Although the town of Langport is some way inland, the port in its name gives us a clue to the fact that it was once a trading centre on the River Parrett. In fact, in Anglo-Saxon times it was as far up the river as sizeable ships could navigate. South-east of the town the river branches into a tributary called the River Yeo, also known as the River Ivel. Around 8 miles upstream from here you arrive at the town of Ilchester, which had been an important Roman settlement. There is evidence that the Romans built quays here to handle the arrival of goods delivered through the waterway.

The Ivel was not a wide river, but when it had adequate water in it boats of some description were able to sail up as far as Ilchester. At times when the water level was low, these boats were unloaded at a place called Pill Bridge, 1½ miles downstream. Here you can still find a seventeenth-century packhorse bridge, which itself replaced an earlier one from the thirteenth century. A warehouse also existed on the site, which was used from 1699 until 1805, mainly housing cargos of coal.

The problem was that all goods being transported by road from the bridge to the town had to pay tolls to the borough of Ilchester. This increased the price of coal to local people. Navigation was also hampered for some boats by the restrictive size of the medieval bridge at Langport itself, the Great Bow Bridge. In an attempt to avoid paying the tolls and have a better system of reaching the wharves at Ilchester, a number of local businessmen conceived the Ivelchester and Langport Navigation to create a canal linking the two towns.

On 22 June 1795, the interested parties, now called the Ivelchester and Langport Canal Company, secured an Act of Parliament, the River Ivel Navigation Act 1795, which authorised the improvement of the River Ivel between Ilchester and Bicknell's Bridge, which lies just to the south-east of Langport on the road between Huish Episcopi and Muchelney. Today there is a stone bridge at the spot which was built in 1829 by the Turnpike Trust, but in 1795 it was nothing more than a footbridge. The Act also provided for a cutting to be made through the town of Langport along the course of an existing drain called the Portlake Rhine. The Rhine, which would be widened, would join the River Parrett at Bicknell's Bridge via a lock. There would also be a lock close to Little Bow Bridge near the centre of the town and potentially five more locks on the route to Ilchester. The Act allowed the proprietors to raise £6,000 by issuing shares and a further £2,000 in loans, if required.

The River Yeo (also known as the River Ivel) at Ilchester, where quays were built as far back as Roman times to handle goods arriving through the waterways. During the Industrial Revolution there were also coal wharves here. (Photo © Henry Buckton)

The River Parrett flooding with ice floes in 1940 around the Great Bow Bridge in Langport. (Photo courtesy of Langport and District History Society)

Most of the money needed for the project had already been promised before the Act of Parliament was obtained, which meant that work could begin almost immediately. The engineer appointed for the project was a local man called Josiah Easton, and good progress was made in the first six months at the Langport end of the scheme. However, costs began to escalate and by October 1796 the company found itself in financial difficulty. By now the £6,000 of share capital had all been spent and although things had gone as planned near Langport, towards Ilchester it was a very different story and little work had been achieved. In 1797, the company decided to clear its outstanding debts and effectively abandon the whole undertaking.

However, that was not the end of the story. A few years later there was renewed interest in improving navigation on the River Parrett, the parts of the Ivelchester and Langport Navigation that had been worked on and other linking waterways. A new generation of local businessmen, notably Vincent Stuckey and Walter Bagehot, obtained the Parrett Navigation and Canal Act in 1836 and formed the Parrett Navigation Company. The Act authorised improvements to the River Parrett below Langport and the construction of a canal at a spot in the parish of Barrington, where Stuckey and Bagehot intended to establish coal and timber yards to supply the local villages. This would become the Westport Canal.

Warehouse on Great Bow Wharf, Langport, in the 1890s. (Photo courtesy of Langport and District History Society)

The company was given powers to raise £10,500 by the issuing of shares and an additional £3,300 from a mortgage if required.

Both the Stuckey and Bagehot families were key players in the development of Langport as a prosperous trading hub. They were not only linked together in business but through marriage as well. George Stuckey, Vincent's grandfather, was the founder of Stuckey's Bank and Vincent would become the first chairman of Stuckey's Banking Company. In his early days Vincent had worked as a clerk at the Treasury in London during the premiership of William Pitt Jr. The family also ran a general merchant company in Langport and owned wharves and warehouses in the town and traded in a range of goods, most notably salt, timber, corn and, of course, coal.

As a result of his impressive connections in both business and society, Stuckey managed to recruit the services of Isambard Kingdom Brunel to act as a consultant on the canal aspect of the intended works. Under his recommendation, William Gravatt was appointed chief engineer for the whole scheme. Among his previous accomplishments, Gravatt had worked under Sir Marc Isambard Brunel on the Thames Tunnel and under Isambard Kingdom Brunel himself as supervisor of the engineering team for the Bristol & Exeter Railway. In Somerset, he would be assisted by Charles Hodgkinson.

Great Bow Wharf warehouse in more recent times. (Photo courtesy of Langport and District History Society)

Stuckey's Bank, Langport. Vincent Stuckey, one of the main backers of the Parrett Navigation, was chairman of Stuckey's Banking Company. (Photo courtesy of Langport and District History Society)

It wasn't long before the work on the River Parrett improvements had exceeded the budget that had been set for it, which led to a second Act of Parliament, the Parrett Navigation Act 1839, under the terms of which the company was permitted to raise another £20,000.

In 1839, the Great Bow Bridge was demolished by the company and rebuilt with the present structure. This was done to allow larger boats to pass beneath it. After this, as well as charging tolls to use the canal, there was an additional toll for trade passing under the rebuilt bridge. Some of the shareholders felt that boat users on the River Ivel should also be charged since the water levels on that river had improved as well, thanks to the work carried out on the Parrett. Two of these shareholders, Philip and Nicholas Broadmead, the latter a solicitor, looked into tracing and buying up the original 120 shares from the Ivelchester and Langport Canal Company, which would enable them to implement tolls on the River Ivel. A meeting was held on 26 September 1843 at the Castle Inn, Ilchester, to discuss this, but nothing seems to have come from it.

By 1853, the company was regularly collecting in the region of £1,440 per annum through tolls on the Parrett Navigation, but by 1857 this had dropped to a meagre £673, and by 1871 it was down to just £347. This was largely as a result of competition from the railways. Struggling to survive, the company paid its final dividend to shareholders in 1872.

With money having run out, maintenance on the waterway was non-existent and infrastructure began to collapse. In the end, on 1 July 1878 the Somersetshire Drainage Act was passed by Parliament, which allowed for the transfer of the Parrett Navigation to the Somerset Drainage Commissioners at no cost. Today navigation on these upper reaches of the River Parrett has largely ceased because of sluices that now operate along its course.

The Great Bow Bridge, Langport, which was demolished and rebuilt in 1839 to allow larger boats to pass beneath it. (Photo courtesy of Langport and District History Society)

8

Westport Canal

The construction of the Westport Canal was first authorised by the Parrett Navigation and Canal Act, which was passed through Parliament in 1836. As has been discussed, the Act gave the Parrett Navigation Company the power to raise the funds needed to improve navigation on the River Parrett and several other linking waterways near Langport. This would enable goods to be ferried to and from this part of Somerset, all the way to the docks at Bridgwater.

Westport is a small hamlet between Langport and Ilminster, each being approximately 5 miles away. So why then was it considered to be a suitable place for the terminus of a canal? In fact, prior to the 1836 Act, Westport didn't even exist. On the wording of the Act, the location is described as follows:

> The making and maintaining a navigable canal from the said River Parrett at its confluence with the River Isle, partly along the bed of the said River Isle, to and across certain closes of land called Middlemoor, and thence through certain old and new inclosures to a close of land in the parish of Barrington, adjoining or near to the turnpike road leading from Ilminster to Langport.

The Act notes that the close of land in question is occupied by a certain John Gibbs. The fact of the matter was that the Parrett Navigation Company, which of course was mainly represented by local businessmen Vincent Stuckey and Walter Bagehot, wanted to establish a coal yard or depot on the site from where they could supply the local villages, while at the same time use the canal to ferry produce such as grain, stone and reeds from the canal basin back along the system. Of course, the alternative to moving coal and other commodities to nearby towns and villages was to pay to use the turnpike roads.

Building a canal in the area had been discussed by local parties even before the advent of the Parrett Navigation Act. When the Chard Canal was being built from 1835 the nearby town of Ilminster was on its planned route. That particular canal would enable the carriage of goods to both Bridgwater and Taunton via its link with the Bridgwater and Taunton Canal. Those planning what would become the Westport Canal, at first approached the

Bridge over the Westport Canal at Westport, taken in 1991. (Photo © Clive A. Brown)

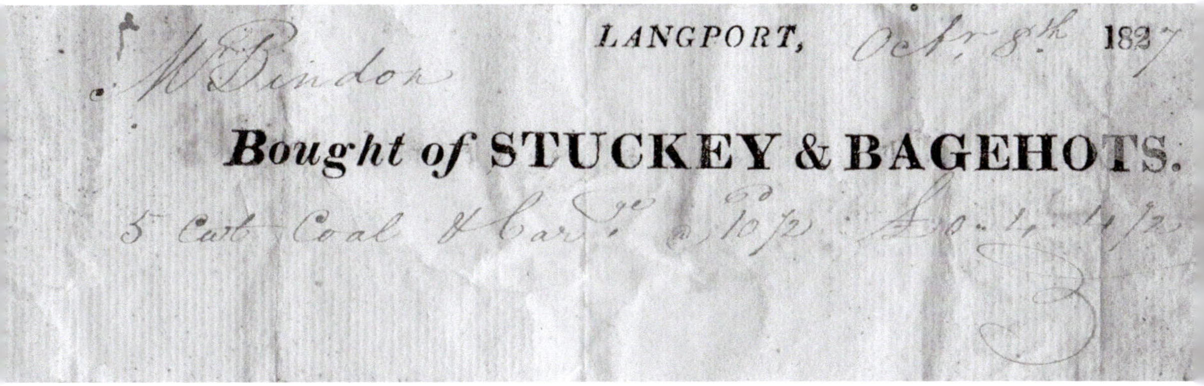

Mr Bindon

LANGPORT, Octr 8th 1827

Bought of STUCKEY & BAGEHOTS.

Receipt for coal bought from Stuckey and Bagehots in 1827. The distribution of coal was one of the driving forces behind the building of the Westport Canal. (Photo courtesy of Langport and District History Society)

Chard Canal Company to see if a link could be established to their system but for whatever reason, their proposal was rejected.

Following this, Stuckey and Bagehot considered an alternative plan of building a canal to meet the River Parrett south of Langport, while also making improvements to the Parrett itself. This eventually led to the passing of the Parrett Navigation and Canal Act in 1836.

Three-storey warehouse built in 1836, which stood next to the canal basin at Westport, photographed in 1991. (Photo © Clive A. Brown)

They also gained the support of the landowners whose land the canal would cut through, notably the Trevillian family and the Combe family. Who actually decided on the name of Westport for the little cluster of buildings that would be established around the canal basin is not known.

With William Gravatt appointed as the engineer for the project, on the recommendation of its consultant Isambard Kingdom Brunel, work on the canal section steamed ahead. Its route from Langport would follow the River Parrett southwards to its junction with the River Isle, where a lock was built. Approximately 1 mile along the River Isle the newly created canal would branch off the river to the south-west, continuing for another 2⅓ miles before finally reaching its terminus at Westport. At the terminus wharves and a basin were built, along with the coal yard, wharfinger's office, canal workers' cottages and warehouses, one of which was used for storing and seasoning timber.

The canal opened for business on 20 May 1839 but almost immediately there were complaints about water levels from some of the merchants using it. In order to remedy the situation, work was needed to remove what are known as shoals from the river section, which are basically an accumulation of sediment that shallows the water. This was sorted out during the following year, after which the canal began to operate smoothly and return a healthy profit for the company.

Being part of the wider Parrett Navigation project, the Westport Canal would decline for the same reasons and over the same period of time as its parent scheme. This led to

Former timber store that was built *c.* 1836 at the entrance to the Westport Canal basin, photographed in the 1990s. (Photo © Clive A. Brown)

the Somerset Drainage Commissioners taking charge of the whole of the River Parrett Navigation at no cost through an Act of Parliament passed on 1 July 1878. In the case of the Westport Canal, in 1880 several of its users presented a petition requesting that the canal be retained in its own right. Unfortunately, the drainage commissioners claimed that they were unable to do this by the terms of the 1878 Act and since its closure the canal has been used as a drain for that part of the Somerset Levels.

To this day the old canal still contains water, thanks to its employment as a drain, and it can be navigated by light craft such as canoes. Footpaths can be followed along its banks and a number of structures associated with the canal survive. At Westport, for instance, there are several buildings dating from 1836 that were built around the canal basin for warehousing, or for the accommodation of canal workers. Near the canal basin entrance is a bridge that takes a track called Barrington Broadway over the canal. Upstream from Westport there are several more surviving bridges to encounter before you finally reach the remains of Midelney Lock, where the canal once joined the River Isle.

Midelney Lock, also known as Muchelney Lock, near the point where the Westport Canal joins the River Isle. (Photo courtesy of Railway and Canal Historical Society)

9

Galton's Canal

All of the canals we have visited so far were built by companies mainly formed from traders, businessmen and political figures, who would benefit from a watercourse arriving at or through their location. There was also, however, a small number that were built by private individuals for their own purposes. A good example of this is Galton's Canal, which

Looking south along Galton's Canal from Westhay Moor Drove. (Photo © Henry Buckton)

was just over 1 mile in length, had one lock in the middle and crossed the moors to the north of the villages of Meare and Westhay, linking the River Brue and the North Drain.

The canal was the idea of a gentleman named Samuel John Galton Jr, a gun manufacturer from Duddeston in Birmingham. In 1790, the peat bogs that then formed part of Westhay Moor were split up into tenements by an Act of Parliament. The land, of which Galton acquired 300 acres, was poor, unimproved and only suitable for cutting into peat blocks, which were then used for domestic heating. However, Galton had a plan to improve his holding and turn it into prime agricultural land.

His plan was to cover the peat with a thick top dressing of good soil. Local people didn't think this would work because from past experience after a short time the top dressing would simply sink down into the peat and be lost. Galton's theory, however, was that if the land was first drained to an adequate level, the loss of the top dressing would not happen and the land would be greatly improved. Once built, the water on the land would drain into the canal.

Looking north along Galton's Canal from Westhay Moor Drove, possibly the lock site. (Photo © Henry Buckton)

Having purchased the land, he was keen to try out his method and employed a local agent from Street called Richard Hammett to manage the project on his behalf. The canal itself, which would be used to carry the vast quantities of soil required, was authorised by the Somerset Drainage Act of 1801 and would be around 1¼ miles long and 16 feet wide. Starting at a junction with the River Brue, the canal would be embanked on both sides for a while, then there would be a small lock that would alter the level of the water to allow the boats to cross the moor. It joined the North Drain at its other end and continued a little further to service land being reclaimed on the north side of the drain.

The North Drain, and for that matter the South Drain, came about because of severe flooding in the area in 1794. As a result of this the Commissioners of Sewers obtained the Somerset Drainage Act through Parliament in 1801. This Act allowed for the improvement of the river system, including the construction of the North and South Drains, which would collect water from the surrounding peat moorlands. Under the terms of the Act, two small canals were actually authorised, Galton's Canal and Brown's Canal, the latter of which little is known about.

The North Drain photographed from Parsons Drove, which came about following severe flooding in the area in 1794. Galton's Canal entered the drain close to the trees on the right. (Photo © Henry Buckton)

The first phase of Galton's operation was to divide his land up into areas of around 40 feet in width, which he called ridges. The peat at the edge of each ridge was dug out and moved into its centre and left for around four or five years until the peat compressed and the surface of the ridge had sunk by about 3 or 4 feet. At this point the ground was already firm enough to support grazing cattle, bearing in mind that this had been a peat bog previously. The cost of this operation was quoted at just over £10 per hectare.

Next, he needed to add the top dressing, and he didn't have to go far to find it: the River Brue itself provided a rich source which was deposited on its banks after heavy rainfall. It is not known exactly when Galton began constructing the canal, but in a paper written by Erasmus Galton in 1845 for the *Journal of the Royal Agricultural Society of England*, soil was first transported on it in 1822, when he notes that 90 cubic yards passed along it. We don't know what the relationship was between the two men, but we do know that Erasmus was a resident of Loxton in Somerset.

Galton's Canal entered the River Brue from a channel to the right of this picture between the two fences. (Photo © Henry Buckton)

In his paper, Erasmus Galton notes that after draining the land the native bog plants that had occupied the moors were soon replaced by ferns. Then, once the top dressing was applied the ferns themselves died away, replaced by clover and meadow grass. All of this was a natural process as no planting or management of the flora was undertaken.

The soil used was largely clay or marl and was added to a depth of 6 feet. Up until 1842, the last year Galton describes, the entire project had cost just over £4,770 and a total of 27,540 cubic yards of soil had been moved along the canal and deposited on the land, which roughly equated to 33,000 tons. The men operating the boats seem to have carried out the whole process and were paid 7*d* a cubic yard for digging the soil out, boating it and landing it.

In 1830, Galton was ordered to repair the flood banks near the canal by the Commissioners of Sewers. The canal appears to have been little used from the 1850s onwards, and it was abandoned in 1897, when the drainage authority constructed a wall across the channel at the point where it entered the River Brue. This included a tidal flap so that water could still discharge into the river at some states of the tide. The canal is now incorporated into the local drainage system. As for the land around it, cattle are still seen grazing in the fields, so his system of land management in a very difficult environment must have worked.

The wall built across the channel of Galton's Canal in 1897 just before it enters the River Brue. (Photo © Henry Buckton)

10

Glastonbury Canal

Surprisingly, Glastonbury, or at least Glastonbury Abbey, had a canal as early as the mid-tenth century to link it to the River Brue at Northover, a distance of just over 1 mile. Its purpose is believed to have been the transport of building materials, but later it was used for delivering goods like grain, wine and fish from the abbey's estate. It is believed to have remained in use until the mid-sixteenth century. Jump forward to the Industrial Revolution and the town would see the construction of another example that ran for 14 miles to the small port of Highbridge.

In the 1750s, Glastonbury became something of a spa town as people believed that the waters from Chalice Well had medicinal properties. However, as the popularity of the spa waned, local businessmen sought different ways to promote their town. The predominant industries were wool and cloth based, but these were in serious decline because of competition from new mill towns in the north of England. Also, in 1794, the area suffered from severe flooding, which brought about the Somerset Drainage Act in 1801. Although this would result in improvements to local rivers and the construction of the North and South Drains, which would collect water from the surrounding peat moorlands and channel it into the River Brue, the town was feeling increasingly isolated and the economy depressed.

In the 1820s, local entrepreneurs began to discuss the possibility of creating a navigable waterway from Glastonbury to the coast which could start to redress the situation. There was also the issue of hefty tolls to pay when using the roads around the town, when bringing coal in and taking locally made goods out.

Two of the main promoters for the canal were brothers Richard and Samuel Prat, who ran a legal firm in the town. Richard was also town clerk. They believed that a canal could bring about an end to the town's economic downturn and called a meeting in August 1825. As a result, Richard Hammett, who had overseen the building of Galton's Canal, was asked to make a survey of the route.

Hammett considered two options, the first of which would simply connect to the River Brue at its nearest point to the town and follow it all the way to Highbridge. This option was rejected mainly on the grounds that it would interfere with the river's drainage function. The second route would involve digging a canal to link into the newly built South

The remains of Glastonbury Canal on its final approach towards the town. (Photo © Henry Buckton)

Drain, which would then meet the River Brue much further along its course before entering a basin and wharf at Highbridge.

Hammett's scheme was eventually adopted and put forward to Parliament which resulted in the passing of the Glastonbury Navigation and Canal Act 1827. The canal company was authorised to raise £18,000 by issuing 360 shares at £50 each, with the power to raise a further £5,000 by mortgage if required. Alternatively, if they were unable to raise enough through the sale of shares, they could borrow any part of the £18,000 from the Exchequer Bill Commissioners.

Construction of the canal began as soon as the company was able to buy the land it needed to link into the South Drain. However, it quickly became evident that Hammett's understanding of canal building was limited, so problems with his survey began to surface. To take things forward, the company decided to approach John Rennie for his advice.

This information board containing an illustration of the canal as it approaches Glastonbury can be found along the public footpath that follows the north bank of the old watercourse close to the town. (Photo © Henry Buckton)

This was John Rennie Jr, the son of the John Rennie, who had already worked on several Somerset canal systems. John Rennie Sr had died in 1821 and his sons John and George were now running his civil engineering business.

Rennie set out several options and the company agreed on building the canal to accommodate boats with a weight of between 40 and 60 tons. This option would also allow the coasters that worked in the Bristol Channel to use the system. He didn't make any changes to the route itself but recommended that two locks and two aqueducts were needed. Rennie costed all of this at £28,720 and, after agreement with the company, work resumed in July 1828.

The construction was plagued by financial difficulties, mainly because the company had failed to raise sufficient funds. The Commissioners of Sewers were unhappy with work taking place at Highbridge, which had effectively stopped in 1830 because, according to them, the contractor had simply 'run away'. The company had also failed to lodge £1,000 with the commissioners, for which they sued in 1831. This was to cover any costs they might incur as a result of the construction of the canal. Even John Rennie threatened to

The South Drain seen from an old railway bridge between Shapwick and Burtle. It was dug out following flooding of the moors around Glastonbury in 1794 and would later become integral to Glastonbury Canal. (Photo © Henry Buckton)

This photograph, probably taken in the 1970s, shows the remains of Shapwick Lock. It was apparently 64 feet by 18 feet and designed to take the coasters that worked in the Bristol Channel. Today, nothing of it survives. (Photo courtesy of Railway and Canal Historical Society: Hugh Compton Collection)

sue, as much of his fee remained unpaid. The cost of construction had risen to £30,000 and in the end the company had no option but to borrow £5,000 from the Exchequer at a rate of 5 per cent.

In spite of the financial difficulties, the canal officially opened on 15 August 1833 amid great celebrations. A cavalcade of boats sailed from Highbridge to Glastonbury and back again. It wasn't until July 1835 that the first cargo moved along the canal, this being a shipment of wood arriving from Canada. However, from the very start the revenue generated by the canal was wholly inadequate and financial difficulties compounded and debts rose.

The finished canal started at a sea lock on what had been the original course of the River Brue at Highbridge. The course of the river had been altered between 1801 and 1809 with the digging of a new cut designed at alleviating flooding in the area. The new cut ended at a clyce, or sluice, which can still be seen today. The canal, however, bypassed the new cut by using the original course of the river to end at the sea lock and wharf. There are no visible remains of the lock today and the wharf area has been redeveloped for housing.

Highbridge Clyce, or sluice, which was constructed when the course of the River Brue was altered between 1801 and 1809. The canal, however, would follow the original course of the river to end at a sea lock and wharf. (Photo © Henry Buckton)

From Highbridge, the course of the canal first followed the River Brue and then the Cripps River until the latter reached Gold Corner, where it meets the junction of the Huntspill River and the South Drain.

From Gold Corner, it followed the South Drain towards Shapwick, where a lock raised the level of the water. The location of Shapwick Lock is by a former iron railway bridge crossing a sharp bend in the South Drain, but nothing now remains of it. From here, the canal split from the South Drain and ran parallel to it, crossing what is now Shapwick Heath National Nature Reserve.

Close to the Railway Inn between Meare and Ashcott, the South Drain turns sharply south under a former railway bridge. At this point the canal crossed the South Drain over a single-arched syphon aqueduct and continued straight ahead towards Glastonbury through what is now Ham Wall Nature Reserve. Some masonry remains of the east abutment of the aqueduct can still be seen.

Eventually, the canal crossed the River Brue via a three-arched syphon aqueduct. Again, this structure has long-since gone, although stone abutments remain along with the remnants of cast-iron plates embedded in the masonry. Finally, the canal made a sharp right-hand turn before reaching a terminal basin located near the old Glastonbury and

Bridge crossing Cripps River, which was part of the Glastonbury to Highbridge navigation. (Photo © Henry Buckton)

Street railway station, which itself is now gone and much of the site is occupied by a timber yard.

In 1840, the Prat brothers, whose legal firm had played a major role in the creation of the canal, were declared bankrupt, leaving the project with a shortfall of over £40,000. Apparently, they had used money from clients' funds to pay some of the construction costs. Richard Prat was removed from office as town clerk and the pair apparently disappeared. Unfortunately, one John Bulleid, a linen draper and shopkeeper in the town, had acted as guarantor on some of the Prats' canal bonds. A writ of summons was served on him, and on the morning of 28 January 1840 he climbed to the top of St John's Church tower, of which he was a warden, and threw himself off, dropping 150 feet to his death.

However, money wasn't the canal's only problem; for instance, because the canal had been built through peat, drainage into it caused the peat to swell. The loss of water reduced the depth of the canal for navigation. As a result, the coasters were unable to use the waterway and their cargos had to be transhipped to smaller boats at Highbridge. This all added to the costs of delivery. By 1848, the canal was only carrying about 4,000 tons of cargo a year, generating an income of around £300, which was unsustainable.

Look carefully at the foliage on the left bank of the South Drain in this picture and you can make out some of the masonry remains of the abutments of the single-arched aqueduct that carried the canal over the drain at this point. (Photo courtesy of David Jury/Somerset Rivers)

In 1848, the canal was sold to the Bristol & Exeter Railway, with the sale authorised by an Act of Parliament passed on 30 June of that year. The shareholders received £7,372 in 1850 and the canal company was dissolved in 1851. Following a further Act of Parliament on 17 June 1852, the railway company was authorised to build a railway between Highbridge and Glastonbury which would be called the Somerset Central Railway. The canal was kept open during the construction of the line and earnt £312 in the year ending September 1853. The new railway largely followed the route of the canal, with much of it built on the existing towpath.

The canal finally closed on 1 July 1854 and the railway subsequently opened on 17 August 1854. By now the locks and aqueducts had been dismantled. Much of the canal is still in water today, as sections of it were given to the Commissioners for Sewers for use as a drainage ditch.

Remains of the abutments of the three-arched syphon aqueduct that carried the canal over the River Brue. (Photo © Henry Buckton)

Sources

'A Brief History of the Somersetshire Coal Canal', Richard Stevens (rtjstevens.co.uk)

'Bridgwater Docks: The Floating Harbour', Bridgwater Heritage Group (bridgwaterheritage.com)

British Listed Buildings (britishlistedbuildings.co.uk) former aqueduct at NGR ST68474874

Chard History Group, 'The Chard Canal', No. 1 (1967)

'Claverton Pumping Station' (claverton.org)

Dorset and Somerset Canal (dorandsomcanal.org)

Galton, Erasmus, 'An Account of Improvement of a Shaking Bog at Meare in Somersetshire', *Royal Agricultural Society of England*, Vol. 6 (1845)

'Glastonbury Canal', Grace's Guide to British Industrial History (gracesguide.co.uk)

'Glastonbury Canal: How the Ill-fated Forgotten Waterway Led to Scandal and Death', *Somerset Live* (somersetlive.co.uk)

'Grand Western Canal History', Tiverton Canal Co. (tivertoncanal.co.uk)

Inland Waterways Association (waterways.org.uk), Grand Western Canal Guide, 2024

'Kennet and Avon Canal', Newbury History (newburyhistory.co.uk)

Linham, Laura, 'Somerset's ill-fated Waterway', Glastonbury Nub News (glastonbury.nub.news)

'Somerset Coal Canal', Timsbury Community (timsbury.org.uk)

Somerset Historic Environment (Somersetheritage.org.uk), Record 15567 and Record 21693

'The Canal', Nynehead Parish Council (nynehead.org)

'The Chard Canal', Off the Beaten Track in Somerset (offthebeatentrackinsomerset.blogspot.com, 2020)

'Vincent Stuckey', Natwest Group (natwestgroup.com)

'Walter Bagehot', Langport Heritage (langportheritage.org.uk)

'Westport Canal', Somerset Rivers (somersetrivers.uk)

'William Gravatt', Iron and Steam (ironandsteam.com)

Acknowledgements

Thanks to the following for permission to use their photographs: Radstock Museum; Derrick Hunt of the Dorset and Somerset Canal Study Group; Miles Kerr-Peterson from the Bridgwater Heritage Group; Nick Higton from the Railway and Canal Historical Society; Janet Seaton from the Langport and District History Society; David Jury from Somerset Rivers; Don Cload; Hugh Llewelyn; Stephen McKay; Rick Crowley; Eirian Evans; Guy Wareham; David Redwood; and Clive A. Brown. Thanks also to Bath in Time for supplying photos credited to Bath and North East Somerset Council and Bath Record Office, Archives and Local Studies.